MW01671193

THISTLES & CROWNS

THE PAINTED CHESTS OF THE CONNECTICUT SHORE

BENJAMIN COLMAN

Foreword by David W. Dangremond

Introduction by Susan P. Schoelwer

Florence Griswold Museum
Old Lyme, Connecticut

This catalogue has been published on the occasion of the exhibition *Thistles and Crowns: The Painted Chests of the Connecticut Shore* (June 7–September 21, 2014) at the Florence Griswold Museum, Old Lyme, Connecticut.

This exhibition has been generously supported by Connecticut Humanities, by The Hartford Steam Boiler Inspection and Insurance Company, and by a group of individuals and restricted funds whose names are cited on page 60. The Museum gratefully acknowledges the generosity of these donors in helping to advance its educational mission.

Copyright © Board of Trustees, Florence Griswold Museum, Old Lyme, Connecticut.
All Rights Reserved.

Library of Congress Cataloging-in-Publication Data

Colman, Benjamin, 1986–
Thistles and crowns : the painted chests of the Connecticut shore /
Benjamin Colman ; foreword by David W. Dangremond ;
introduction by Susan P. Schoelwer.
pages cm
"This catalogue has been published on the occasion of the exhibition
Thistles and Crowns: The Painted Chests of the Connecticut Shore
(June 7/September 21, 2014) at the Florence Griswold Museum,
Old Lyme, Connecticut."
Includes bibliographical references and index.
ISBN 978-1-880897-26-3 (alk. paper)
1. Painted furniture--Connecticut--Exhibitions.
2. Chests--Connecticut--Exhibitions. I. Florence Griswold Museum. II. Title.

NK2703.C65 2014
749'.3--dc23

2014017886

PHOTOGRAPHY Paul Mutino
DESIGN Jack Design
PRINTING Puritan Capital, Hollis, New Hampshire

Florence Griswold Museum
96 Lyme St.
Old Lyme, CT 06371
www.FlorenceGriswoldMuseum.org

FRONT COVER
Chest, ca. 1710–1730, Old Saybrook Historical Society.

BACK COVER
Chest (detail), ca. 1710–1730, Webb-Deane-Stevens Museum, Wethersfield, CT.

FRONTISPIECE
Detail from John Goodwin, *An Exposition of the Ninth Chapter of the Epistle to the Romans* (London: Printed by John Macock, 1653), 2.

OVERLEAF
Chest (detail), ca. 1710–1730, Old Saybrook Historical Society.

CONTENTS

FOREWORD

From the time of its founding in 1936, the decorative arts of New England have had a strong presence at the Florence Griswold Museum in Old Lyme, Connecticut. The museum was established in large part to preserve the magnificent 1817 house built on Lyme Street by Samuel Belcher for William Noyes. With its grand Grecian portico supported by stately Ionic columns, the house was an appropriately ambitious architectural statement for that prominent Old Lyme family, and later became the home of prosperous sea Captain Robert Griswold when he purchased the property for his wife Helen in 1841. It was there that they would raise their three daughters Florence, Louise, and Helen Adele, and son Robert Jr. Today the house is filled with furniture and objects artfully assembled from original and period furnishings to evoke the turn of the century era when Miss Florence Griswold opened her home to some of the most important painters of the day. Under her watchful eye and benevolent spirit, the Old Lyme art colony flourished in the early years of the twentieth century as cosmopolitan artists discovered the joys and inspiration of country life.

At the same time as prominent contemporary artists from New York and Boston were seduced by the charm of Old Lyme's landscape, historic houses, and meandering country roads, relics of Connecticut's colonial past were being rediscovered as long-neglected furnishings were unearthed from dusty attics and musty basements in shoreline towns like Old Saybrook and Guilford. These historic treasures enjoyed newfound recognition in renowned museums and important private collections. Notably, in 1909 The Metropolitan Museum of

Chest with Drawer, 1710-1730
Made in Guilford, CT. Oak, pine, tulip poplar; paint.
H: 43 1/4 in. W: 47 in. D: 20 1/4 in.
Webb-Deane-Stevens Museum, Wethersfield, CT.
Gift of Mr. and Mrs. Ellsworth Grant, 1973.2

Art acquired two beautifully painted Connecticut chests (pp. 46-47), then thought to have been made in Guilford, their surfaces richly resplendent with exuberantly colored compositions of bright flowers, curling vines, prickly thistles, red and white roses, and *fleurs-de-lis*. Other prominent museums quickly followed suit.

Although these painted chests have long been considered icons of New England's vernacular furniture, they have also presented a conundrum to scholars of American design. Their forms are eclectic, ranging from joined chests to high chests. Their painting is eccentric, featuring symbols of the British crown during a period when tradition tells us Connecticut colonists developed an independent American spirit. Now scattered across the country in major collections, a sizable group of these related painted chests has not been seen side-by-side since 1957 when the Connecticut Historical Society displayed six of them within a larger exhibition of early Connecticut chests. Over the last century these chests have been variously associated with the towns of Saybrook or Guilford as research and scholarship has evolved. For many years they were attributed to the shop of Saybrook cabinetmaker Charles Guillam, a native of the Isle of Jersey. Based on painstaking research and keen observation of surviving examples, this exhibition and catalogue take a fresh look at the construction and painting of these chests to offer important new evidence of a wider circle of shoreline craftsmen and artisans responsible for these distinctively decorated chests.

It is fitting that these chests are coming home to the Connecticut shore for a renewed look and reinterpretation in this exhibition, returning to the same landscape where their story began in the early eighteenth century. The Florence Griswold Museum is deeply grateful to The Metropolitan Museum of Art, the Wadsworth Atheneum Museum of Art, the Henry Francis du Pont Winterthur Museum, the Henry Whitfield State Museum, the Webb-Deane-Stevens Museum, and the Old Saybrook Historical Society for lending their treasured chests to the exhibition. By bringing together this select group of distinctively decorated chests, Florence Griswold Museum Assistant Curator Benjamin Colman explores and decodes the complex story of their construction, decoration, use, and history, providing important new insights into the origins of these iconic and widely admired examples of early American decorative art.

David W. Dangremond

Vice President and Collections Committee Chair
Florence Griswold Museum
and
St. Anthony Hall Professor of Art History
Trinity College

Chest with Drawer, right side detail, 1710–1730. Made in Guilford, CT. Oak, pine, tulip poplar; paint. Henry Whitfield State Museum, Guilford, CT. Gift of Mr. Wilbur Pardee, 59.1919

INTRODUCTION

The publication of this beautifully illustrated catalog pays testimony to the enduring fascination that a small group of early eighteenth-century Connecticut furniture pieces have held for collectors and scholars of American decorative arts and material culture. Distinguished by colorful flowers, vines, birds, architectural details, and, most notably, roses, thistles, crowns, and *fleurs-de-lis*, these painted chests and chests of drawers were avidly sought by early collectors, and they subsequently found their way into major Americana collections around the country.

I first encountered the painted chests of coastal Connecticut as a graduate student in the Winterthur Program in Early American Culture. Fresh from the Midwest, I had never been north or east of Pennsylvania, and New England was a *terra incognito*. Learning about early New England furniture meant memorizing details of furniture construction and design (which to my untrained eye seemed virtually indistinguishable) and matching them to town names (which as yet had no grounding in history or geography). Plymouth, Taunton, Hadley, Wethersfield, New Haven, Milford … the list of towns seemed endless, the inventory of forms at once bewilderingly varied and yet distressingly similar. How was one to make sense of it all?

And then I came upon Winterthur's vibrant painted high chest (pg. 7), generally recognized as the culminating example of the group. Here, at last, was something that stood out from the crowd, a furniture type that I could confidently recognize, with an attribution and a story that was easy to remember. By the mid-1970s, when I studied at Winterthur, the chests formerly known as "Guilford chests" had been rechristened "Saybrook-Guilford chests," linked to the workshop of Charles Guillam. Long thought to come from a non-Anglo background (Walloon or French), Guillam was subsequently traced to Jersey, an English-owned but French-speaking island in the English Channel off the coast of Normandy. Gratifyingly, Guillam's French-speaking heritage provided a tidy explanation for the furniture's distinctive appearance, enabling the recurring *fleur-de-lis* to function as both an emblem and a welcome mnemonic device for its presumed lineage.

In the years since first meeting with Saybrook-Guilford painted furniture, I have spent much time exploring Connecticut's rich visual and material culture and the fascinating histories of its towns and peoples. For more than a decade, it was my privilege to have an unparalleled perspective on Connecticut's past, as curator of the extraordinary holdings of the Connecticut Historical Society in Hartford. As I studied the collections, considered acquisitions, answered queries, and researched family lineages,

I accumulated considerable knowledge of the state's cultural history, best understood as the aggregate of many distinct local histories. Because of what I have called Connecticut's "persistent localism," the furniture and other arts and artifacts produced in the state are not easily contained within a single statewide narrative; rather one must move beyond regionalism to investigate the interwoven stories of individual towns and villages, and the movements of people, ideas, and goods within and between them.

Over the past four decades, numerous closely focused furniture studies have mined this approach, using a combination of documentation, provenance, and painstaking object examination and analysis to situate particular groups of objects in specific communities at specific (if sometimes broadly defined) time periods. Geographically-based surveys have investigated furniture produced in towns along the Connecticut River, while other projects have drilled into the woodworking output of specific towns or explored conditions of production for particular clusters of furniture.

The Saybrook-Guilford furniture has largely fallen outside the scope of these various studies. Political jurisdictions separated these two towns from an early date, with Guilford turning eastward, along the shore, to become part of New Haven County. Saybrook looked northward, joining the Connecticut Colony centered in Hartford, later split off to become part of Middlesex County. Study of New Haven Colony furniture has focused on the seventeenth-century style, excluding the early eighteenth-century painted chests of Saybrook-Guilford. Connecticut Valley studies generally extend no further south than Haddam, where the river enters a narrow gorge and a line of hard, crystalline rock separates the upriver towns from the coastal settlement at Saybrook. Ironically, although Saybrook is located at the mouth of the Connecticut River, it has generally been regarded as outside the scope of Connecticut River Valley studies.

The current catalog thus represents a welcome addition to the literature on Connecticut furniture, in turn enhancing our understanding and appreciation of New England material culture and American decorative arts more broadly. Although the total census of Saybrook-Guilford pieces numbers only about two dozen, they are widely scattered. By bringing together six examples, *Thistles & Crowns* offers an opportunity to trace the progression from traditional joined chests to new-fangled, board-constructed case pieces, and to compare and contrast the handling of decorative details. The diversity of forms, construction techniques, and decorative approaches, Benjamin Colman argues, all point to "a range of shops and makers" and "the development of a short-lived regional style." Setting aside questions of Charles Guillam's possible authorship and French-speaking heritage, Colman situates the painted furniture at the nexus of historical traditions of woodworking and access to trans-Atlantic culture, just as Saybrook itself lay at the confluence of the Connecticut River and Long Island Sound. Listings of woodworking tools recorded in probate inventories between 1720 and 1747 point to as many as seventeen craftsmen who could have been Guillam's colleagues or competitors.

Colman also turns a fresh eye on the painted motifs that serve as hallmarks of the Saybrook-Guilford chests, but also their most elusive feature, their origins and meanings tantalizing and mystifying generations of collectors and scholars. The roses, thistles, and *fleurs-de-lis* are immediately recognizable as emblems of the kingdoms of England, Scotland, and France. Early writers associated these motifs with the Stuart rulers of seventeenth-century England, consequently dating the chests no later than 1660. As subsequent furniture scholarship re-dated the furniture forms to the early eighteenth century, the roses, thistles, lilies, and crowns came to be interpreted as vestigial motifs, shorn of earlier political significance. Colman firmly rejects this purely decorative interpretation, arguing that these motifs offer multiple layers of meanings "hiding in plain sight," drawing upon heraldry, British imperial identity and royal ambitions, botanical illustrations, coinage, printer's ornaments, and traditional folk beliefs.

Consideration of the decorative motifs leads to questions about the practices of ornamental painting in colonial New England. Small clusters of early eighteenth-century painted furniture survive with associations to a number of towns, for example, the painted Japanned case pieces of Windsor, Connecticut, or the vine-painted examples of Taunton, Massachusetts, attributed to Robert Crosman. Intriguingly, Crosman is identified in primary documents principally as a drum maker, an occupation that suggests training in ornamental painting. This circumstance in turn suggests the possibility of a more complicated dynamic for the production of painted furniture: rather than assuming that a single shop was responsible for both construction and decoration, are variations the result of interactions between multiple painters as well as woodworkers?

Early tavern signs provide an instructive parallel, being similarly composed of wooden forms and painted decoration. Surviving examples from the eighteenth and early nineteenth centuries reveal considerable disparities between woodworking and painting skill sets on individual signs: well-constructed examples may be crudely painted, while roughly made signs may display assured ornament. Is it pure coincidence that three of Connecticut's earliest known tavern signs derive from the same locality as the Saybrook-Guilford chests, or perhaps evidence of a persistent local tradition of decorative painting? The signs for Bull's Inn, Centerbrook (1749), Hayden's Inn, Essex (1762), and Kirtland's Inn, Saybrook Point (ca. 1771) were all created for establishments within the eighteenth-century town of Saybrook. Shared construction methods, related turnings, and the use of the same molding plane to shape the horizontal rails point to production in the same woodworking shop or shop tradition. However, the painted decoration just as clearly manifests different hands, with the fully-rigged ship and British coat of arms on the Hayden sign being far more complex and sophisticated than the black horses shown in profile on both sides of the other two signs.

It has been a pleasure to reconsider the Saybrook-Guilford chests from the perspective of several years' immersion in Connecticut history. Although it seems unlikely that new examples will emerge at this date, one never knows. In the meantime, questions generated by the present study point the way to fruitful future research. And because so few examples remain today in the region where they originated, *Thistles & Crowns* offers local residents an exciting opportunity to celebrate a vibrant form that is likely to be unknown to many.

Susan P. Schoelwer
Robert H. Smith Senior Curator
George Washington's Mount Vernon

Dover
Exeter
C. Elizabeth
Hedeek
R. Pascataway
Portsmouth
Hampton
Amsbury
Haveril
Salesbury
Newbury
Andover
Wamesick
Bradford
Rowly
Ipswich
Wenam
OF
C. Ann
Glocester
Manchester
Beverly
Salem
WE
Dierfield
Squaheeg
Chelmsford
Billireca
Shosheen
Ridin
Hatfield
Swanfield
Northampton
Hadlay
Lancaster
Concord
Woburn
Malden
Westfield
Springfield
Marlbrough
Charles T.
Marble Head
ORK
Sudbury
Cambridg
Boston
Lynn
Windsor
Worcester
Medfield
Hull
Hingam
Roxbury
Dorchester
Milton
Braintrie
Weymouth
Scituate
Mendon
Hartford
Marshfield
C. Cod
Wethersfield
Duxbury
Uncas
Providence
Seaconck
Swansey
Bridgwater
Plymouth
A
Middletown
Warwick
Norwich
Taunton
East Ham
Eastham
Say broke
New haven
Milford
Shatford
Fairefield
Chichester
Stanford
Greenwich
Merrenick
New London
Sand:wich
Barn:stable
Wickford
Menimoy
Lime
Yarmouth
West Chester
Stonyton
Ports:mouth
Nantuket
Guildford
Brentford
Newport
Rode I.
Midleburg
Egerton
Martins Vinyard

CONSTRUCTION

The region between Guilford and Saybrook sits on the Connecticut shore of Long Island Sound. During the colonial period, these two waterways served as important conduits for the exchange of culture and commodities. This fact is demonstrated by the beautiful and beguiling painted chests made in these towns in between 1700 and 1740. Alternately called *Guilford Chests, Saybrook Chests,* or *Saybrook Guilford Chests* as thought about the roughly 25 surviving examples has evolved over the past century, these chests exhibit patterns of construction and richly polychrome painted surfaces that reflect both the cultural heritages of the region, and the sensitive integration of fashionable styles carried from Europe by oceanic trade. Working with familiar tools and techniques, the craftsmen responsible for these chests created useful objects for their communities indicating a distinctly local adaptation of a transatlantic style.

GUILFORD AND SAYBROOK The historic towns of Guilford and Saybrook encompassed a 20 miles stretch of the Connecticut coast of Long Island Sound settled as part of the earliest wave of English colonization in New England (Fig. 1). Bound on the east by the tidal marshes at the mouth of the Connecticut River, Saybrook traces its roots to the short-lived Saybrook Colony (1635–1644) established as a strategic fortification by John Winthrop, Jr. (1606–1676), son of John Winthrop (1588–1649), Governor of the Massachusetts Bay Colony. Following a contentious decade, leadership of the Saybrook Colony transferred to the larger Connecticut Colony in 1644.[1] Guilford traces it earliest settlement to 1639, when a small group of English colonists arrived, largely yeomen farmers from the English counties of Kent and Surrey.[2] By the early eighteenth century, the towns of Killingworth and Durham had been formed near these initial settlements.

1 Edward Well (English, 1667–1727), *A New Map of the Most Considerable Plantations of the English in America*, detail of Long Island Sound and the Connecticut River Valley, 1700–1738. Ink and watercolor on laid paper. Courtesy of Historic Deerfield, Deefield, MA. Gift of Mrs. June Lauzon, 1996.44.

Although each of these towns has a distinctive history, they are part of a larger trajectory of colonization along the coasts and inland waterways of New England. Shortly following the earliest New England settlements of Plymouth (1620), Salem (1626), and Boston (1630), a proliferation of small communities began throughout New England. In Connecticut, the ease of travel by water relative to the difficulty of overland transit saw the development of towns along two axes. The Connecticut

River provided access to fertile farmland and natural resources in the north, and Connecticut Colony towns formed at Windsor (1633), Wethersfield (1634), Hartford (1635), and Springfield (1636; governance transferred to the Massachusetts Bay Colony in 1640). The coast of Long Island Sound, with access to intra-colonial and international trade, eased the settlement of New Haven (1638), Milford (1639), Stratford (1639), and Branford (1644) in modern Connecticut. Across the Sound on Long Island, Southampton (1640), Southold (1640), and East Hampton (1648) were established during this same period.

For several reasons the historical background of these two towns is germane to an understanding of the painted chests made there in the early eighteenth century. The historic tradition of woodworking carried to these towns at their seventeenth-century founding set a precedent that continued to inform carpenters and joiners working there in the eighteenth century. Additionally, access to coastal waterways and oceanic trade brought Connecticut cabinetmakers into contact with new styles, materials, and furniture forms as they developed in larger colonial ports and in international style centers. If the painted chests from Saybrook and Guilford were rooted in the past, they also looked to the freshest ideas of their own time.

CONNECTICUT TRADITIONS Situated on two different waterways with distinctive patterns of culture, the towns of Guilford and Saybrook developed identities that straddle the line between the close-knit communities of the towns lining the Connecticut River in the seventeenth century, and the comparatively open coastal communities ringing Long Island Sound that had regular contact with Dutch settlements around Manhattan. The residual influence of both regional traditions

2 *Chest*, 1650–1680. Made in New Haven Colony, possibly Guilford. White Oak. H: 28 11/16 in. W: 50 9/16 in. D: 24 5/16 in. Yale University Art Gallery, New Haven, CT. Mabel Brady Garvan Collection, 1930.2265.

is evident in the painted chests made in Saybrook and Guilford. The earliest seventeenth-century woodworking from these towns—shaped by the late-medieval tradition of carpentry carried to North America by English colonists[3]—continued to inform the construction of these chests.

When these painted chests were rediscovered by modern collectors of American historic furniture in the early twentieth century, they were dubbed "Guilford Chests" in reference to the town where the first example was studied by scholars.[4] Guilford was a suitable place of origin in many respects for modern scholars attempting to make sense of a diverse tradition of chest forms with a shared ornamental treatment. The seventeenth-century furniture traced to Guilford was well regarded by early collectors and scholars. Objects like this ca. 1640–1680 oak joined chest demonstrate the direct transplantation of vernacular English traditions of carpentry and joinery to colonial New England during the seventeenth century (Fig. 2). There are several distinctly English features of this chest. It is constructed entirely of white oak while related examples use red and white oak alongside a broader range of woods. Both the back and top are framed with multiple oak panels, where other examples use broad boards of pine to serve the same function with less labor. The carved decorative motif—a "double heart"—traces its roots to Gloucestershire in England in the same period.[5] This type of joined oak chest evolved slightly over the course of the seventeenth century, and a similar pattern of construction and decoration is seen in chests made in Guilford in the later years of the century (Fig. 3). There are some formal differences between the earlier and later chests. The overall proportions changed slightly with time. The lid on the later chest is a not framed, but made of four boards attached with a cleat. White oak was

3 *Chest*, 1640–1680. Made in Guilford, CT. White oak, Chestnut. H: 28 9/16 in. W: 50 1/2 in. D: 21 15/16 in. Yale University Art Gallery, New Haven, CT. Bequest of Charles Wyllys Betts, B.A. 1867, 1887.5.

4 *Chest with Drawer*, 1710–1730. Made in Guilford, CT. Oak, pine, tulip poplar; paint. H: $32\frac{5}{8}$ in. W: $45\frac{1}{4}$ in. D: $20\frac{1}{4}$ in. Henry Whitfield State Museum, Guilford, CT. Gift of Mr. Wilbur Pardee, 59.1919.

5 *Chest with Drawer* (back detail), Henry Whitfield State Museum, Guilford, CT. Gift of Mr. Wilbur Pardee, 59.1919.

6 *Chest with Drawer* (left side detail), Henry Whitfield State Museum, Guilford, CT. Gift of Mr. Wilbur Pardee, 59.1919.

7 *Chest with Drawer* (right side detail), Henry Whitfield State Museum, Guilford, CT. Gift of Mr. Wilbur Pardee, 59.1919.

still the primary wood used for visible elements of the chest, but the boards were more carefully worked into thinner stock and chestnut was used as a secondary wood.[6] These chests and a small group with related carving were celebrated by early collectors for their connections to the earliest settlers of the town, and often came with histories of ownership by prominent citizens.

Given that strength and local longevity of the late-medieval carpentry tradition, it is easy to trace a clear lineage between the earliest chests joined in Guilford, and the early eighteenth-century painted chests from the same region.

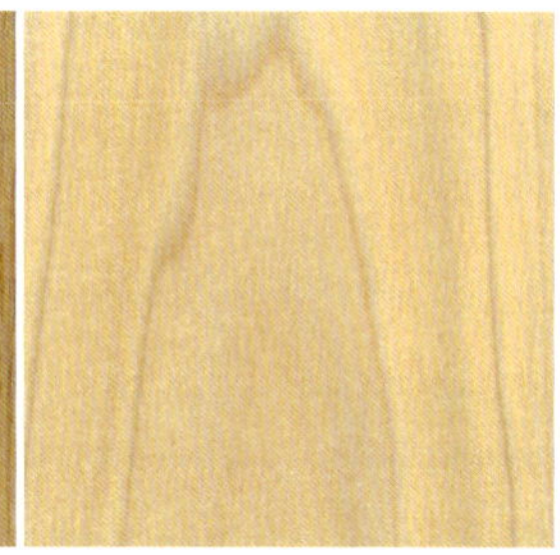

8 Red Oak (*Quercus rubra*)

9 Eastern White Pine (*pinus strobus*)

10 American Chestnut (*Castanea dentata*)

11 Tulip Poplar (*Liriodendron tulipifera*)

12 American White Ash (*Fraxinus americana*)

The painted chest (Figs. 4–7) now at the Henry Whitfield State Museum survived into the twentieth century with a history of ownership in Guilford and East Guilford, modern Madison.[7] Like some of the surviving Saybrook-Guilford chests, this example demonstrates the slow evolution of craftsmanship traditions in small Connecticut communities like Guilford.[8] Like the earlier examples from the same town, it was constructed with a riven oak frame joined together with mortises and tenons, but other elements show a changing sensibility. The panels are made of pine with tapering, chamfered edges that sit securely within the oak frame. The lid is made of tulip poplar. Instead of a series of panels across the front used as a surface for repeated courses of ornamental carving, the large single panel serves as a ground for a painted composition of scrolling leaves, vines, and blossoms.

It was a logical development for New England carpenters and joiners to incorporate diverse woods into their furniture. If a tradition of solid oak furniture came from rural England, North American forests provided a ready supply of different species suitable for different uses in furniture making. Oak continued to be used to frame chests of this style, given its useful ability to neatly split from a log into joinable planks with a wedge and hammer, but milled pine (white and yellow), chestnut, tulip poplar, ash, and cedar were also used (Figs. 8–12). Well-documented histories of trade and harvest in Guilford exist for most of these species during the colonial period, with town meeting and court records providing thorough evidence for the appropriate use—and censurable misuse—of lucrative resources in the

13 *High Chest*, ca. 1710-1727.
Made in Saybrook or Guilford, CT.
White pine, tulip poplar, ash; paint.
H: 54 3/4 in. W: 40 1/8 in. D: 21 in.
Courtesy Winterthur Museum, Wilmington, DE. Bequest of Henry Francis du Pont, 1957.1110.

forests surrounding the town. As early as the 1681 the town enacted a fine for the improper harvest and use of cedar trees from "cedar swamp out of the town."[9]

NEW IDEAS FROM THE WIDER WORLD Despite the clear link between Guilford's earliest furniture and eighteenth-century pieces like the chest illustrated in figures 4–7, the larger group of chests from Saybrook and Guilford includes a diverse range of forms and different patterns of construction. Unlike the joined chests, forms like the high chest of drawers from the Winterthur Museum's collection show the different ways that joiners, carpenters, and cabinetmakers in Saybrook and Guilford kept abreast of new styles (Fig. 13). Constructed of white pine, tulip poplar, and ash, this high chest shows that the cabinetmaker used a very different set of skills than the craftsmen who created the related joined chests. Unlike the framed chests, the high chest was built with a smooth case using broad boards securely dovetailed together. The structural integrity of this new approach to cabinetmaking—dovetails rather than mortises and tenons, solid cases rather than joined frames—allowed the maker to explore new decorative elements on expansive surfaces. The six turned legs were shaped on a lathe, and raise the chest up to the imposing height that made it a commanding, decorative presence in a Connecticut home.

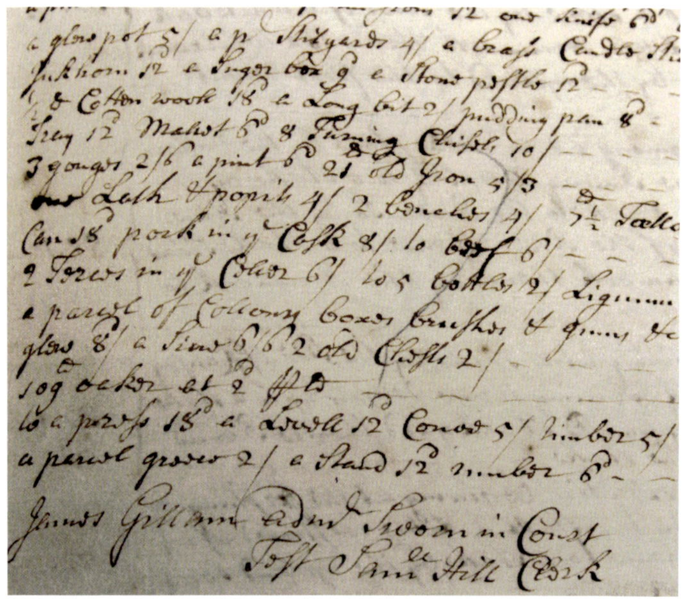

The form of this piece, a high chest of drawers, was a recent development in colonial Connecticut in the early eighteenth century. The form was introduced to colonial North America in the 1690s,[10] and its presence in Saybrook or Guilford shortly thereafter highlights the awareness of recent fashions in these small communities. The new form presented both challenges and opportunities to furniture makers. While a cabinetmaker in the larger town like Boston, Newport, and Philadelphia might have used walnut, maple, mahogany, or another richly figured wood, the craftsman in Connecticut who made this piece took advantage of a regional taste for polychrome paint seen on simpler forms from the same towns.

In the 1930s, the Winterthur high chest was attributed to the shop of a Saybrook cabinetmaker named Charles Guillam (1671–1727) based on details from the 1727 probate inventory of his estate. In 1935 historian Gilman C. Gates published a history of nearby Old Saybrook, and included a rough transcription of Charles Guillam's 1727 probate inventory as evidence of his profession (Fig. 14). His name alternately spelled Guillame, Gyllam, and Gillam, he was an immigrant cabinetmaker of French heritage originally from the English island of Jersey.[11]

14 **Detail of Charles Guillam's estate inventory, August 23, 1727. Guilford Probate vol. 2, p. 201. Guilford / Madison Probate Court, Madison, CT.**

When Guillam died in Saybrook, his workshop included books on architecture and design, two unfinished chests of drawers, a "great chair," a "carved chair," and "a painted chest with drawers." The inventory also mentions a large selection of woodworking tools that included two workbenches, bench hooks, molding planes, a mortising chisel, carpenter's chisels, a scraper, several vises, a variety of saws, and a glue pot among a long list of implements. Although basic carpentry tools are found in many period household inventories of yeoman farmers, specialized tools like these indicate a trained cabinetmaker earning a living from the craft. The inventory also listed, "a parcel of collours," "boxes, brushes & gum," and "109 lbs. oaker," proving that he had the tools needed to both construct and paint a piece of furniture.[12]

Bolstered by the historical evidence of this inventory, scholars for many years attributed the painted chests to his shop. No longer "Guilford Chests," they were redubbed "Saybrook Chests," and Guillam's shop was associated with the diverse forms, methods of construction, and types of painted ornament they show. More recently, scholars have explored Guillam's heritage in the French-speaking English Channel Islands by comparing the Saybrook and Guilford painted chests to their contemporaries from that region with provocative results.

There are several reasons why the Guillam attribution is misleading. Charles Guillam certainly owned the tools to produce chests like these, but there is no immediate evidence that he actually did other than proximity to an eighteenth-century owner of one chest.[13] He may have made one of them. He may have made several of them. He certainly did not produce all of them. The painted decoration on one example includes the date 1730, three years after Guillam's death. Other hands were clearly at work.[14]

The diversity of form and construction seen in the surviving painted chests indicates a range of shops and makers. Some, like the monumental high chest (Fig. 13), were carefully built into a neatly elevated case. This was a modern form for the period, made by a cabinetmaker trained in new techniques and styles. Others, like several diminutive boxes, were roughly nailed together. The joined chest illustrated at the beginning of this chapter took a well established form from the region, and updated it with a novel painted finish. Although histories of ownership for these chests are rare, it is unclear why chests with strong provenances in towns separated by 20 miles would have been made in the same shop when their form and decoration is so different.

Instead of stretching the material evidence of these painted chests to fit what is known about Guillam, there is a simpler explanation for the simultaneous similarity and variety seen within the chests illustrated in this book. These beautiful pieces of furniture were not created by a single hand, or in a single town, but instead show the development of a short-lived regional style along the Connecticut shore of Long Island Sound in the first decades of the eighteenth century.

This explanation is supported by surviving evidence in the probate records from the towns of Guilford, Killingworth, Durham, and Saybrook from the period of 1720–1750. Probate inventories provide an important window into the material life of different historic periods. Taken to tally the value of a deceased individual's estate in order to settle his debts and distribute any remaining assets, these inventories include detailed descriptions—and monetary values—for the contents of an estate. When a woodworker died, this often included a description of his tools. Guillam was far from the only furniture maker working between Guilford and Saybrook during this period, and many other hands contributed to the surviving painted chests from these towns.

OTHER WOODWORKERS Charles Guillam's competitors in the nearby towns of Killingworth, Durham, and Guilford included a range of craftsmen. Many were active in more than one trade. In addition to carpentry, nearly all were engaged in farming and husbandry. Several owned shoemaker's tools. Many were literate, as evidenced by the selection of religious and secular books recorded in inventories. As with their contemporaries, wooden furniture and carpentry tools were of relatively modest value in eighteenth-century inventories when compared to textiles and real estate.

The carpenters and woodworkers named here do not constitute a definitive list. Others remain to be identified, and regional contributions were certainly made by journeyman cabinetmakers and carpenters who worked on the Connecticut shore but removed to a different region by the time of their death. Such craftsmen are not reflected in probate records.

Nevertheless, it is useful to identify a broader group of carpenters working around Saybrook and Guilford in the early decades of the eighteenth century. The list that follows below identifies some of the men working in these towns who may have been capable of producing chests of this type.

Ebenezer Bishop (1707–1747) of East Guilford owned both carpenter's tools and joiner's tools when he died.[15]

John Brooker (1695–1731) was born in Guilford but died in Saybrook. His inventory listed a small selection of "his Carpenter's tools," "shoemaker's tools," and "husbandry tools."[16]

Daniel Buckingham's (1672–1725) August 1725 estate inventory in Saybrook included an extensive list of chests, boxes, chests of drawers, along with a "carv'd chest" and "carv'd box." The inventory also records "Joyners Tools" valued at over £4.[17]

Samuel Buell (1641–1720) was born in Windsor, CT, and was a proprietor of Killingworth at its founding. He owned extensive lands in what is now the town of Clinton. His August 1720 inventory included a small group of carpenter's tools, a "turning gouge," and "turning tooles."[18]

Samuel Bushnell (1645–1727) of Saybrook owned "carpenters tools" alongside his books, bedding, and husbandry tools in his February 1727/28 inventory.[19]

William Bushnell of Saybrook (1680–1733) owned an extensive list of tools when he died, divided on his inventory into two categories: "Carpenter's tools," and "Joyner's Tools." The carpenter's tools included handsaws, a mortising ax, a square, carpenter's rule, chisels, and draw shaves. His joiner's tools included finishing planes, fine chisels, and a turning lathe.[20]

Joseph Chittenden of Guilford (1672–1727) owned a mortising chisel, several saws, and other woodworking tools when he died.[21]

Caleb Dudley of Guilford (1673–1730) owned both cooper's tools and carpenter's tools.

John Fenner of Saybrook (died 1733) owned "Joyner & Carpenters Tools," a "shoe makers Bench & tools," and a "barber's box" when he died.[22]

John Fosdick (1693 /94–1747) of Guilford owned a "chest & drawers painted" when he died, a small selection of carpenters tools, and unused pine boards.[23]

John French of Guilford's (1652–1727) estate included "old carpenters" and "old coopers" tools when he died, along with a "large joynter" for smoothing board edges, a spoke shave, and chisels.[24]

Captain Janna Meigs (1672–1739) of East Guilford owned both a "painted box," and a selection of woodworking tools when he died. It is unknown whether his painted box was of this type, or if it was of his own production. His tools include basic carpenter's tools, but many are specified as cooper's tools.[25]

George Lee of Saybrook (died 1726) owned a small group of chisels, saws, a square, and a compass when his estate was inventoried.[26]

Nathaniel Lynde (1692–1749) of Saybrook owned cooper's and carpenter's tools when he died.[27] His father is discussed in chapter three.

Nathaniel Pratt (died 1744) of Saybrook owned both "joyners" tools and cooper's tools when he died. His household inventory included a "carved work chest of draws," "carved work box," "varnisht chest," "large chest with turnd feet," "chest varnisht with turnd ft."[28] In period text, "varnisht" or "varnished" was used to refer generally to painted or coated surfaces—a face covered in makeup might be referred to as "varnisht"—rather than the modern term denoting a clear finish. If these chests came from his own workbench, it would indicate a single craftsman producing a wide variety of decorative finishes—carved ornament, decorative turned elements, and varnished or painted finishes—in Saybrook during the period when the surviving painted chests were made.

Zachariah Sanford (1695–1732) of Saybrook owned a long list of saws, squares, compasses, augurs, planes, chisels, and turning tools.[29]

Thomas Stanley of Durham (died 1723) was removed from the coast by several miles in a small town founded by families pushing north from Guilford in 1699. His inventory included woodworking tools recorded as "Carpenters Tools," "Drawing knife," and "Tennon Saw." It also includes paints and pigments, recorded as "Painted papers," "Colouring Stuff," and "a Jarr of Linseed oyle."[30] Although no conclusive link between Stanley and a painted chest survives, this inventory provides evidence of woodworkers contemporary to Guillam with the tools to both construct and paint furniture.

Joseph Stone of Guilford (died 1733) owned unspecified "joyner's tools" in his inventory.[31]

A wide community of woodworkers was active in Saybrook, Guilford, and the adjacent towns in the early decades of the eighteenth century. This fact is reflected in the diversity of the surviving furniture from the region in a range of styles. Many of the above listed men possessed the tools and possibly the know-how to make the furniture that has been attributed in the past to Charles Guillam.

As new information continues to come to light, it may be possible for future scholars to discover fruitful connections between woodworkers, ornamental painters, and surviving pieces of furniture.

NOTES

1 *Saybrook's Quadrimillenial* (Deep River, CT: Press of Clark & Smith, 1886), 10–16.

2 Ralph Dunning Smith, *The History of Guilford, Connecticut* (Guilford, CT: J. Munsell, 1877), 9–14.

3 Philip Zea, "Chest," cat. 71 in Gerald W.R. Ward and William N. Hosley, Jr., ed. *The Great River: Art & Society of the Connecticut Valley, 1635–1820* (Hartford: Wadsworth Atheneum, 1985), 193.

4 Ethel Hall Bjerkoe, "Charles Gillam–Cabinetmaker," *Spinning Wheel* 29:4 (May 1973), 24–25.

5 Gerald W.R. Ward, *American Case Furniture in the Mabel Brady Garvan and Other Collections at Yale University* (New Haven: Yale University Art Gallery, 1988), 84–86.

6 Patricia E. Kane, *Furniture of the New Haven Colony: The Seventeenth-Century Style* (New Haven: The New Haven Colony Historical Society, 1973), 46–49.

7 Henry Whitfield State Museum curatorial files, 59.1919. Guilford, CT.

8 Martha Willoughby, "From Carved to Painted: Chests of Central and Coastal Connecticut, c. 1675–1725," 1994. Master's thesis, Winterthur Program in Early American Culture, University of Delaware, 1–4.

9 Bernard Christian Steiner, *A History of the Plantation of Nenunkatuck and of the Original Town of Guilford, Connecticut* (Baltimore: Published by the author, 1897), 180–182.

10 Ward, *American Case Furniture*, 235.

11 Robert F. Trent, "A Channel Islands Parallel for the Early Eighteenth-Century Connecticut Chests Attributed to Charles Guillam," *Studies in the Decorative Arts* 2:1 (Fall 1994), 77–80.

12 Gilman C. Gates, *Saybrook at the Mouth of the Connecticut* (Orange, CT: Press of the W.H. Lee Co., 1935), 182. Charles Gillam estate inventory, August 23, 1727. Guilford Probate vol. 2, 200–201. Guilford/Madison Probate Court, Madison, CT.

13 Bjerkoe, "Charles Gillam—Cabinetmaker," 24–25.

14 Christie's, New York, *Property from the Collection of Mrs. J. Insley Blair* (Sale 1618), Lot 521, Jan. 21, 2006.

15 Ebenezer Bishop estate inventory, January 25, 1747/48. Guilford Probate vol. 4, 411–415.

16 John Brooker estate inventory, 1731. Guilford Probate vol. 2, 443–444.

17 Trent, "A Channel Islands Parallel," 80. Daniel Buckingham estate inventory, May 11, 1725. Guilford Probate vol. 2, 42–44.

18 Samuel Buell estate inventory, August 9, 1720. Guilford Probate vol. 1, 13–19.

19 Samuel Bushnell estate inventory, February 16, 1727/8. Guilford Probate vol. 2, 254–255.

20 Trent, "A Channel Islands Parallel," 80. William Bushnell estate inventory, August 25, 1733. Guilford Probate vol. 3, 79–84.

21 Joseph Chittenden estate inventory, November 15, 1727. Guilford Probate vol. 2, 227–229.

22 John Fenner estate inventory, September 4, 1733. Guilford Probate, vol. 3, 87–90.

23 John Fosdick estate inventory, August 25, 1747. Guilford Probate vol. 4, 377–379.

24 John French estate inventory, February 15, 1727/28. Guilford Probate vol. 2, 248–250.

25 Janna Meigs estate inventory, June 5, 1739. Guilford Probate vol. 4, 36–39.

26 George Lee estate inventory, November 1, 1726. Guilford Probate vol. 2, 131–132.

27 Trent, "A Channel Islands Parallel," 80.

28 Nathaniel Pratt estate inventory, September 6, 1744. Guilford Probate vol. 4, 215–220.

29 Trent, "A Channel Islands Parallel," 80. Zachariah Sanford estate inventory, November 13, 1732. Guilford Probate vol. 3, 33–36.

30 Thomas Stanley estate inventory, May 23, 1723. Guilford Probate vol. 1, 149–153.

31 Joseph Stone estate inventory, August 6, 1733. Guilford Probate, vol. 3, 85–87.

DECORATION

The inventive polychrome painted decoration on the Saybrook and Guilford chests quickly captivates the eyes and minds of modern viewers. Filled with bold colors, exuberant compositions, and curious images, the whimsical beauty of this tradition tells a complicated story about the culture of coastal Connecticut in the early eighteenth century. Created in keeping with the tastes of the period that favored an integration of form and lush ornament, these chests represent a distinctly local expression of a Baroque style that originated in Europe and came to North America through exported luxury goods and immigrant craftsmen. The unique painted iconography reflects both the political climate across the young British Empire, and the emergence of distinctive traditions in different colonial towns. Made of inexpensive materials harvested in abundance from New England forests, these chests stand testament to the ingenuity of colonial craftsmen as they created fashionable objects for demanding consumers using the skills and tools they had at hand.

Distilling diverse influences from around the world into beautiful motifs, the painting on these chests reflects the complex local cultures of the Connecticut shore in the early eighteenth century.

PAINTING AND ORNAMENTATION Decorative painting on furniture was used from the very beginning of colonial woodworking in the seventeenth century, and was one tool in a sophisticated kit used by carpenters, cabinetmakers, and joiners to create beautiful and desirable pieces of functional furniture. Carefully selecting woods for specific purposes based on their strength, ease of use, and visual qualities, a joiner considered which surfaces would be visible on a piece of furniture. Carpenters, joiners, and cabinetmakers were careful to utilize some woods on the surface of a piece—like oak, riven to reveal patterns of grain and ray tissue from the log—while less decorative woods like chestnut were relegated to drawer bottoms and backs where they would not be seen daily.

Carved ornament allowed a joiner to explore decoration as both a visual and tactile quality, and appears on the earliest surviving Connecticut furniture.

1 *Chest with Drawer*, 1710–1730. Made in Guilford, CT. Oak, pine, tulip poplar; paint. H: 43 1/4 in. W: 47 in. D: 20 1/4 in. Webb-Deane-Stevens Museum, Wethersfield, CT. Gift of Mr. and Mrs. Ellsworth Grant, 1973.2.

Although uncommon in extant examples, decorative inlay was produced in the New Haven Colony as early as the 1660s by craftsmen who composed careful patterns from thin-strips of wood glued to the surface of a piece of furniture.[1] Turned elements were used as both purely decorative features when applied to a surface, or as functional ones when incorporated into a leg for a chair, table, or high chest.

2 *Chest with Drawer* (back detail), 1710–1730. Webb-Deane-Stevens Museum, Wethersfield, CT. Gift of Mr. and Mrs. Ellsworth Grant, 1973.2.

3 *Chest with Drawer* (right side detail), 1710–1730. Webb-Deane-Stevens Museum, Wethersfield, CT. Gift of Mr. and Mrs. Ellsworth Grant, 1973.2.

4 *Chest with Drawer* (left side detail), 1710–1730. Webb-Deane-Stevens Museum, Wethersfield, CT. Gift of Mr. and Mrs. Ellsworth Grant, 1973.2.

Ornamental painting was an important tool for carpenters and joiners across New England who used it to represent images, emulate the appearance of expensive tropical woods like ebony or mahogany, and unify the appearance of different species of wood with a single color. These different ornamental techniques were not used in isolation, and often complement one another on complicated pieces of furniture.

The painted chests made between Saybrook and Guilford highlighted in this study all use paint as a pictorial tool—that is, the painting depicts specific images rather than abstract geometric pattern or *trompe-l'oeil* emulation of expensive materials. They can be divided into two groups.

The first group includes examples like a joined chest (Figs. 1–4) now in the collection of the Webb-Deane-Stevens Museum which predominantly incorporate a generalized language of vegetal decoration. Although much altered by early efforts at restoration in the twentieth century that removed some of its ground color, this chest retains in passages the painted images of its original decoration. The large central panel on the front of the chest was composed with vertical symmetry

5 *Posset Pot*, ca. 1710–1725. Possibly made in London or Bristol, England. Tin-glazed earthenware. H: 7 9/10 in. W: 5 9/10 in. Victoria and Albert Museum, London, UK. Bequeathed by Miss D.B. Simpson, Slindon, Sussex. C. 50&A-1977.

6 *Caudle Cup*, ca. 1690–1713. Made in New York, N.Y. Silver. H: 5 3/4 in. W: 5 7/8 in. Wt: 23 oz., 1 dwt. Yale University Art Gallery, New Haven, CT. Anonymous gift for the John Marshall Phillips Collection, 1953.10.2.

around a central vessel—a two-handled cup not unlike ceramic versions imported to North America from Europe (Fig. 5), and the silver versions created by colonial silversmiths (Fig. 6)—painted with a pin-wheel blossom growing from the aperture. A vine scrolls to both the left and right, sprouting a variety of leaves and blooms in different colors. As in this chest, thistles are sometimes incorporated into the pictorial vocabulary.

The second category includes a wider variety of forms like the chest of drawers in the collection of the Wadsworth Atheneum (Fig. 7) and a nearly related example at Historic Deerfield (Figs. 8–10) with a specific set of politically charged icons that include thistles, Tudor roses, *fleurs-de-lis*, and crowns among the rich imagery of their painted surfaces. While it is not known who owned the chest in the colonial era, the historic meanings of the signs and symbols that adorn it reveal many things. On each side panel, monumental tulips sprout from small hillocks represented by two ogee curves similar to rural Connecticut River Valley architectural pediments of the same period.[2] Each course of drawers on the front is given its own painted treatment. The inner corners of the two small upper drawers each feature the foliate-head of the so-called *Greenman*. Derived from pre-Christian English folk lore and religion, these foliate heads were common features on medieval English church architecture dating to the thirteenth century.[3]

The second level features flowering vines not unlike those present in the first category. The third is arranged around a two-handed bowl holding a flower and several vines. Two small thistles curl back towards the center of the drawer, and two striped birds perch in profile on either side of the center. The lower drawer is composed around a large *fleur-de-lis* in the center, on which two birds perch in profile as above. The leaves of the *fleur* gradually transition from a solid color into a striped vine that curls outward. Each vine sprouts two red tulip blossoms, a red-and-white rose blossom, and a large upright thistle among other elements. A crown surmounts each thistle and the *fleur-de-lis.*

7 *Chest of Drawers*, 1705–25. Made in Saybrook or Guilford, CT. Oak, tulip poplar, pine. H: 43 in W: 44 1/4 in. D: 20 1/2 in. Wadsworth Atheneum Museum of Art, Hartford, CT. Wallace Nutting Collection. Gift of J. Pierpont Morgan, 1926.327.

8 *Chest of Drawers*, 1705–1725. Made in Saybrook or Guilford, CT. Oak, tulip poplar, pine, chestnut, yellow poplar; paint. H: 43 1/2 in. W: 44 1/2 in. D: 19 1/2 in. Courtesy of Historic Deerfield, 1956.302. Photo by Penny Leveritt.

9 *Chest of Drawers* (left side detail), 1705–1725. Courtesy of Historic Deerfield, 1956.302. Photo by Penny Leveritt.

10 *Chest of Drawers* (thistle detail, lower drawer), 1705–1725. Courtesy of Historic Deerfield, 1956.302. Photo by Penny Leveritt.

When Charles Guillam's 1727 estate inventory was discovered by modern antiquarians in the 1930s, the inclusion of paints and painter's tools sparked a connection to chests like those illustrated. Yet the information recorded in that inventory that relates to painting is extremely spare. It lists, "a parcel of collours," "boxes, brushes & gum," and "109 lbs. oaker."[4]

Such information is helpful, but far from conclusive. To begin with, the most substantial listing is for a remarkable quantity of ocher, a ferric-oxide-based pigment used for a range of warm browns. The volume of that pigment suggests it served a wider use in his shop beyond decorative pictorial painting. This idea is supported by both physical and documentary evidence. In estate inventories from Connecticut shore towns in the early eighteenth century, *brown chairs* are common entries, and surviving examples of both chairs and chests retain traces of an overall coat of a warm brown used to visually unify an object made of many types of wood.

The more relevant contents of Guillam's inventory, the "parcel of colors" is unhelpfully obscure. Like Thomas Stanley's 1723 inventory from Durham discussed in the first chapter that included "colouring stuff" and linseed oil, these documents can only tell a modern reader that different pigments were in active use, but do not specify what those pigments were. Helpfully, the 1739 inventory of Lewis Lyron of Milford, Connecticut (1650–1738), included a long list of pigments that he probably sold and mixed himself. They included "Spanish brown," "verdegrease," "Red Oak," "yelow oaker," "white lead," and "Read lead."[5]

Technical analysis of the painted surface on these chests identifies the presence of these pigments on surviving examples. When samples from the painted motifs on the high chest (pg. 7) were analyzed, the following pigments were detected (Fig. 11): vermilion, orpiment, verdigris, blue verditer, carbon black, lead white, and mars red.[6] In some examples the painted decoration is laid out in three courses. The overall pigment for the ground is first applied in a uniform coat. Then the design for the pictorial images is laid out in lead white. Finally, the polychrome paint is brushed over the lead white under-painting.[7] While the ground color bleeds into

the grain of the woods for decorative effect, amplifying the natural refractivity of the wood in direct light, the under-painted decoration sits slightly proud of the surface in crisply opaque colors.

Recent technical analysis and archival documents both serve to reiterate an important feature of these chests. Although their painting has dulled with age, when new they featured a rich array of pigments in fantastical compositions. Their coloristic vibrancy both delighted the eye—appealing to the tastes of the day favoring complex ornament and rare materials collected from across the globe—and captivated the mind—highlighting the signs and symbols painted in bright colors against a dark ground for clarity and emphasis.

COLONIAL BAROQUE The European Baroque style emerged in the wake of the Renaissance, and was characterized in architecture and design by what art historian Erwin Panofsky termed "a lordly racket." In the wake of the Italian Renaissance that reprised the forms and proportions of the classical world, an exuberant style emerged to toy with that stolid historicism and invigorate design with an expressive approach to ornamentation. Dynamic forms, complex surfaces, theatricality, bold contrasts, and eclecticism took the place of geometric purity.[8]

11 These modern colors approximate the bold hues the historic pigments would have had when newly applied.

12 *Chair*, ca. 1705–1715. Made in London, England. Walnut; cane. H: 55 6/10 in. W: 18 9/10 in. D: 21 9/20 in. Victoria and Albert Museum, London, UK. Bequeathed by Dr. C.J.N. Longridge, W57-1952.

13 *Chest of Drawers*, 1653. Made in England. Oak with cherry, bog oak, ebony, ivory, snakewood, brass, and mother-of-pearl. H: 49 1/5 in. W: 46 in. D: 24 1/2 in. Victoria and Albert Museum, London, UK. 657:1 to 8-1883.

14 *Dressing Table*, ca. 1754. Designed by John Linnell (1729–1796); Made by William Linnell (1698–1763), London, England. Pine and Mahogany with Japanned decoration. H: 37 3/4 in. W: 56 7/10 in. D: 28 1/2 in. Victoria and Albert Museum, London, UK. W.55:1 to 24-1952.

This style manifested in different ways in both architecture and design in England. In furniture it marked a rise of elaborate carved ornament on objects like this high-backed chair with a woven cane seat (Fig. 12), a growing interest in tropical hardwoods used to compose striking contrasts in color and grain on a piece of furniture (Fig. 13), and decorative painting called Japanning used to emulate the appearance of imported Asian lacquered furniture (Fig. 14). In ceramics it encouraged a vogue for expensive Asian porcelain (Fig. 15) painted with bold scenes and patterns in many colors, which influenced European ceramics when English and Continental potters emulated that style in tin-glazed earthenware (Figs. 16 & 17). In textiles a taste developed for so-called "Bizarre" silks woven in contorted, abstract patterns (Fig. 18). Printed cotton made in India for European export used ornamental compositions filled with blossoms, vines, and leaves (Fig. 19) evocative of those subsequently found on English-made textiles (Fig. 20). Although this Baroque style found its purest expression in seventeenth-century Continental design, it also reshaped English style, and its influences came to New England through a variety of channels.

Imported prints and books brought the latest European styles to North America during this period. As evidenced by Charles Guillam's inventory, discussed in the previous chapter, that included a book on architecture, these texts found their way into the hands of craftsmen looking for inspiration and new ideas. Printed portraits of political figures and cultural leaders were imported into the colonies, often based on works of the most important Baroque painters active in England; Flemish painter Anthony van Dyck (1599–1641) (Fig. 21) and German painter Sir Godfrey Kneller (1647–1723) (Fig. 22) never travelled to North

15 *Plate*, ca. 1740. Made in China. Porcelain with cobalt underglaze. Diam: 8 7/8 in. Florence Griswold Museum. Gift of the Old Lyme-Phoebe Griffin Noyes Library, the Evelyn MacCurdy Salisbury Ceramics Collection, P. 1974.99

16 *Dish with Thistle Ornament*, ca. 1707. Probably made in London or Brislington, England. Tin glazed earthenware. Diam: 12 in. Victoria and Albert Museum, London, UK, Given by Mr. Stuart G. Davis, C.58-1925.

17 *King William Dish*, ca. 1690–1700. Probably made in England. Tin glazed earthenware. Diam: 11 1/2 in. Florence Griswold Museum; Gift of the Old Lyme-Phoebe Griffin Noyes Library from the Evelyn MacCurdy Salisbury Ceramics Collection, P1974.5

18 *Dress Fabric,* detail, ca. 1708. Made in Spitalfields, London, England. Silk damask brocaded with colored silk. H: 65 in. W: 21 1/4 in. Victoria and Albert Museum, London, UK, 711-1864.

19 *Palampore*, ca. 1700–1725. Made in the Coromandel Coast, India. Dyed cotton chintz. H: 81 9/10 in. W: 78 in. Victoria and Albert Museum, London, UK, IS.18-1976.

20 *Dress Panel,* detail, 1725–1750. Made in England. Silk embroidered with silk and gold thread. H: 46 in. W: 41 1/2 in. Victoria and Albert Museum, London, UK, Given by Miss J. Shaw-Preston, T.270-1969.

America, but engravings after their portraits helped to shape the portraits made in New England.[9]

New England consumers imported fashionable goods from around the world, and these imported objects informed the pieces Connecticut craftsmen produced. While shipping manifests and newspaper advertisements can reveal certain aspects of this exchange, the personal stories of colonial New Englanders striving to keep up with new styles from a distance can be more difficult to discern.

In February 1719/20, the Rev. Samuel Sewall of Boston (1652–1730) sent a letter to his cousin's son in London, the merchant Samuel Storke, requesting the purchase of new furnishings. Storke made a special and profitable practice of trading with English colonists in North America. He was closely related to the Sewall family in Boston through their mutual roots in the southeastern English village of Romsey, and had spent two years in Boston from 1712 to 1714 learning about colonial trade and developing lucrative friendships with prominent families.[10] He was also well connected in New York, trading with Philip Livingston (1686–1749) of Livingston Manor in the Hudson Valley, who sent his sons to apprentice with Storke in London.[11]

These connections made him a wealthy merchant in London, but also gave his taste a certain measure of authority when dealing with his friends, family, and customers in North America. When Sewall wrote to Storke in 1720, he requested a long list of fashionable goods to be purchased for his daughter Judith Sewall (1702–1740) in anticipation of her May 1720 marriage to the Rev. William Cooper of Boston (1684–1743). Sewall's request reveals much about English colonists' cultural ambitions and uncertainty when pursuing the latest fashions. He asked for "curtain and vallens for a Bed," with "Bases, if it be the fashion." He requested a

21 *Kenelm Digby*. Engraved by Robert van Voerst (1597–1636) after Anthony van Dyck (1599–1641). Yale Center for British Art, New Haven, CT. Paul Mellon Collection, B1977.14.10505.

22 *Queen Anne*, 1702. Printed by John Smith (1652–1743) after Sir Godfrey Kneller (1646–1723). Yale Center for British Art, Yale Art Gallery Collection, New Haven, CT, Library Transfer, Gift of John Hay Whitney, B1994.4.426.

"looking glass of black walnut frame of the newest fashion (if the fashion be good)." He ordered a fireplace fender "of the newest fashion," and brass candlesticks "of the newest fashion," along with an extensive list of goods for a home that includes pewter dishes, glass cups, and 12 high-back cane chairs.[12]

Samuel Sewall was a wealthy minster in Boston well connected to the most prominent citizens of that town. Yet his dealings with a London merchant illuminate the relationship between fashionable New Englanders and their European agents. Knowing that his family needed to keep homes in the latest style but unaware of what that style might be, he deferred to Storke to interpret the latest London fashions for him, and send along suitable goods.

Those goods included objects like the cane chair illustrated in figure 12, a high-backed chair with a woven seat that presented ample opportunities for a carver to embellish functional elements with carved acanthus leaves, dramatic curves, and a theatrically arched crest. Chairs like that English example were imported to New England in great quantities, and inspired carpenters across the region to develop their own take on the style. What emerged were objects like this New England chair, ca. 1720 (Fig. 23), that are clearly rooted in a European precedent, but used different materials and ornamental carving.

The process of translating a European style for New England consumers gave colonial craftsman many opportunities to offer their own interpretation to suit local tastes. Painted with bold colors and rich with natural imagery, the Saybrook and Guilford chests clearly emerged from the fashionable impulse for the Baroque. Although the expression of that impulse from Saybrook and Guilford is unique, different clusters of colonial craftsmen in small communities developed distinctive local reactions to an international Baroque style in the late-seventeenth and early-eighteenth centuries. Craftsmen in flourishing ports like Boston or Newport responded directly to fashionable goods in the latest styles, facing competition from goods like those imported by Sewall, and incorporated new forms and decorative motifs into their work to keep up with consumer tastes. Their counterparts in rural towns like Hadley, Massachusetts, Wethersfield, Connecticut, and Taunton, Massachusetts, were aware of the same styles, but found novel ways of incorporating new influences into their workshop for the small communities they served.

23 *Side Chair*, ca. 1720. Possibly made in coastal Connecticut. Maple, ash; rush seat. H: 42 in. W: 13 in. D: 19 1/2 in. Florence Griswold Museum, Gift of Mrs. Neva Johnson, 1984.23.

The so-called Hadley Chests were among the first traditions of American vernacular design to achieve widespread recognition in the nineteenth century (Fig. 24). They carry the name Hadley Chest for the town of Hadley, Massachusetts, where an example was first identified, but were in fact made in many towns along the banks of the Connecticut River between Hartford, Connecticut, in the south, and Deerfield, Massachusetts, in the north. These chests are identified by the iconic tulip-and-vine patterns carved along the rails and stiles of the old-fashioned chest frames. This type emerged in the last quarter of the seventeenth century, and remained in production through the 1730s. Most examples would have been painted in the period, either a single color or a variety of colors, but many do not retain their original paint.[13]

A related tradition also appeared in Wethersfield, Connecticut, in the so-called "Sunflower chests" (Fig. 25) possibly associated with the shop of Peter Blin (1640–1725). These sunflower chests were made roughly between 1675 and 1725, and are identified by the carved flowers on their panels with concentric rings of petals that seem to represent a generalized image of a rosette. Richly carved and embellished with applied turned ornaments, these chests were also painted in a variety of colors when new.[14]

In Taunton, Massachusetts, from the late 1720s to the early 1740s the carpenter Robert Crosman (1707–1799) created a similarly distinct group of

24 *Chest with Drawer*, 1670–1710. Made in the Connecticut River Valley. White oak, yellow pine. H: 33 1/4 in. W: 45 in. D: 18 5/8 in. Yale University Art Gallery, New Haven, CT, Mabel Brady Garvan Collection, 1930.2190.

painted chests that use linear ornament over a dark ground in a limited tonal range (Fig. 26). Painting birds, vines, blossoms and inscriptions, he created allover decorative compositions on simply joined chests with drawers.[15] Crosman is also tellingly identified as a drummaker in the period where his trade would have involved the painting of company insignias on instruments for local militias. This type of painting would have been more complex and polychrome in execution than the painting that survives on chests attributed to his shop, and it suggests a clear link between painting on furniture and the broader practice of ornamental painting in the period. This tradition also suggests, as Susan Schoelwer notes in her introduction, that furniture scholars may find fruitful information by looking at the wider communities of craftsmen in colonial towns where interesting objects survived. Known as both a carpenter and drummaker, Robert Crosman's training in Taunton was not that of a joiner or cabinetmaker. Perhaps the distinctive painting on the Saybrook and Guilford chests owes its roots to a similar craftsman, heretofore unidentified, with a training in the visual arts rather than furniture making.

These three traditions of vernacular Baroque furniture in New England all share several important features with the painted chests made in Saybrook and Guilford. All were small communities, but were accessible by major waterways. Wethersfield, Hartford, Deerfield, and Hadley are all on the Connecticut River, and the deep waters of the Taunton River flow into Narragansett Bay. The importation of goods, immigration of people, and circulation of ideas kept these communities aware of new developments in fashionable tastes, but without the density of wealth found in major colonial ports like Boston, Newport, or New York, craftsmen were free to develop vernacular adaptations of those tastes.

If the wealthiest citizens of these small towns could purchase expensive goods from Europe or from other colonies, a joiner serving the general population in a small town was wise to work with a diverse set of tools. The distinctive colonial expressions of Baroque taste that emerged during this period reflect the central contradiction of these different groups of chests. If craftsmen and consumers were familiar with new styles, removed from urban centers and with limited financial resources, they were also free to experiment with idiosyncratic responses using familiar tools.

25 *Chest with Drawers*, 1670–1710. Attributed to Peter Blin, Wethersfield, CT. White oak, yellow pine, maple, cedar. H: 40 in. W: 47 5/8 in. D: 21 3/8 in. Yale University Art Gallery, New Haven, CT, 1800.4.

26 *Chest with Drawer*, 1731. Attributed to Robert Crossman, Taunton, MA. White pine; paint. H: 32 in. W: 35 1/2 in. D: 17 1/4 in. Yale University Art Gallery, New Haven, CT, Gift of Jane and Gerald Katcher, LL.B. 1950, 2013.57.1.

THISTLES, ROSES, LILIES, AND CROWNS Why did thistles, crowns, *fleurs-de-lis*, roses, tulips, and birds appeal to Connecticut colonists in the early-eighteenth century?

When Malcolm A. Norton wrote about the then-called "Guilford Chests" in the August 1922 issue of *The Magazine Antiques*, he looked to the thistles, crowns, roses, tulips, and *fleurs-de-lis* painted on these chests to help date them. Correctly noting the associations all of these symbols had with the seventeenth-century

Stuart kings of England, he argued that the chests could have been made no later than 1660 by "an ardent Loyalist, living in or near Guilford" around the time of the English Civil War.[16] The thistle, a hardy plant known to thrive in harsh conditions, was a national symbol of Scotland carried to London by the Stuarts. The rose, abstracted from the red and white Tudor rose, was an icon of the English monarchy. The *fleurs-de-lis*, a stylized lily flower still an emblem of modern France, had been for centuries an icon of the French monarchy. It is based on those associations that the distinctive painting of the Saybrook and Guilford chests was dismissed as an anachronistic holdover from the seventeenth century. Yet those old symbols acquired new meanings in colonial Connecticut as the British Empire took shape in the early-eighteenth century. Following the 1707 Acts of Union, a unified Great Britain was formed from the Kingdoms of England and Scotland. This was not always a peaceful process, and it took place during an extended period of political instability in England and international conflict across Europe. Scottish dissenters regularly arose against British rule in the first half of the eighteenth century in a series of Jacobite rebellions. English monarchs claimed historic dominion of France in the period. European wars of royal succession found their way to North America as Queen Anne's War (1702–1713), King George's War (1745), and the French and Indian War (1754–1763). In the extended wake of the English Civil War (1642–1651), Interregnum (1649–1660), and Glorious Revolution (1688–1689), new iconographic combinations emerged to buttress the uneasy position of new monarchs with familiar symbols of national identity and power. These iconographies found modern uses for old symbols.

Images like thistles, roses, crowns, and *fleurs-de-lis* had long histories of circulation in North America. The images that found their way onto the Saybrook and Guilford chests probably first appeared in New England at the time of its first colonization on coins like this silver halfgroat piece minted in London under James I between 1607–1609 (Fig. 27). Dubbed the "Thistle Crown" in the period, like several of the chests here illustrated, it featured multiple crowns. The union of the two—on one side, the Scottish thistle, on the other, the concentric petals of the English Tudor rose—was an important gesture in the seventeenth century, placing icons of both kingdoms on the same coin in symbolic unity under a single crown. This combination appeared in different places throughout the seventeenth century. Ornamental designs of thistles, crowns, roses, and *fleurs-de-lis* appeared printed in books in the seventeenth century (frontispiece),[17] and it is likely that texts decorated with these images found their way to New England.[18]

27 *Silver Halfgroat Piece of James I*, 1607–1609. Minted in London. Silver. Diam: 7/10 in. Yale University Art Gallery, New Haven, CT, transfer from Sterling Memorial Library, Yale University, Gift of Thomas H. Johns, B.A. 1818, 2001.87.21216.

A thistle was not just a thistle in the British Empire. William Salmon's (1644–1713) *Botanologia: The English Herbal, or History of Plants,* published 1710–1711,

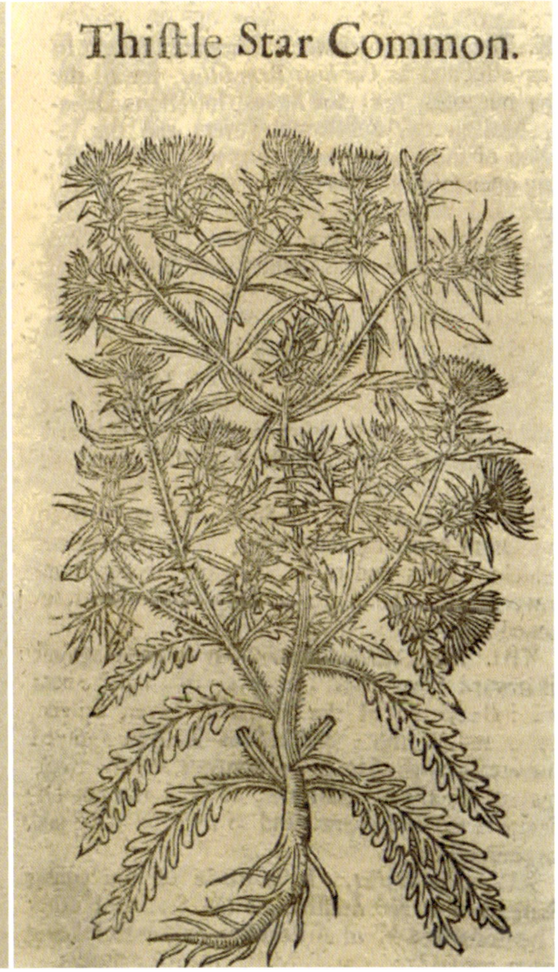

recorded the physical and practical attributes of dozens of species of the plant (Fig. 28 & 29). The book includes chapters dedicated to Common Thistles, Wild Thistles, Woolly Thistles, Blessed Thistles, Melancholy Thistles, Ladies Thistles, Star Thistles, and others. He described the Common High Way Thistle with leaves of pale green, the dense Thistle Upon Thistle considered the "most Prickly Thistle," the Gentle Way Thistle "thin set with prickles," the Asses Farting Thistle so named for obvious reasons, and the White Thorn Thistle that grows "on almost every Ditch and Bank-Side."[19]

Salmon recommended putting the different varieties to different uses. For common thistles, he advised, "that if any bald place be Bathed with the Juice, it causes the Hair to grow again speedily" and a strong brandy brewed with the whole plant could be used "to resist a Cold Scurvy."[20] The juice of the Great Melancholy Thistle was said to "potently open Obstructions of the Spleen, Liver, Reins and Womb."[21] A "Posset-Drink" of powdered White Thorn Thistle seeds "mixed with a little Mull'd Canary, or White Port Wine," was prescribed for "Hypochondriack Melancholy, Scurvy, Dropsy, Jaundice, and Gout."[22] Although ubiquitous on the

28 *Thistle Upon Thistle*, 1710. Wood engraving as printed in William Salmon, *Botanalogia*, 1138.

29 *Common Star Thistle*, 1710. Wood engraving as printed in William Salmon, *Botanalogia*, 1150.

British countryside, the different species of the plant were attributed extraordinary curative properties.

The potent plant also carried significant political ramifications in the early eighteenth century. The Scottish Order of the Thistle, which by legend traces its roots to a ninth-century Scottish King Achaius, was revived in 1687 by King James II shortly before the Glorious Revolution ended his reign. The revived Order included a medal featuring in an engraving by the Bohemian artist Wenceslaus Hollar (1607–1677; active in London 1637–1677), a crowned thistle (Fig. 30). The Order fell dormant during the reign of King William and Queen Mary (1688–1702), but was revived in 1703 by Queen Anne, who increased the number of Knights of the Thistle from 8 to 12.[23] Using the Order to help cement her support among the Scottish nobility during a period when rebellion fomented among Stuart Loyalists, she helped make the thistle not only a symbol of Scotland, but also an icon of the British monarch.

Although the king or queen could not be in all corners of the British Empire at once, the ruler's symbols could establish a royal presence in distant settlements like Saybrook and Guilford in Connecticut.

The power of the humble thistle worked its way into many facets of colonial life. In 1712, the Rev. Cotton Mather wrote a letter to John Woodward of the Royal Society in London outlining a number of North American botanical cures for common illnesses. He included a new suggestion for treating the swelling of the lymph nodes due to tuberculosis. Scientists in the period referred to this swelling as scrofula, but it carried the common name of *King's Evil.* During the eleventh-century reign of Edward the Confessor in England (1003–1066), a belief developed that only the touch of the king could cure *King's Evil.* This belief survived into the eighteenth century. During Queen Anne's reign, sufferers of the illness travelled to St. James's Palace for the cure. After being examined by a doctor to verify their symptoms, they were touched by the Queen. This curious cure was sometimes

30 Wenceslaus Hollar (1607–1677), *Design for a medallion for the Order of the Thistle.* Made in London. Engraving on paper. The Thomas Fisher Rare Book Library, University of Toronto, Wenceslaus Hollar Digital Collection.

doled out en masse: on March 20, 1712, Queen Anne was reported to have cured 200 sufferers of the ailment with her touch at a public healing. Among those who claimed a cure in this fashion were the author Samuel Johnson, who suffered from the illness as a young boy but retained, "a solemn recollection of a lady in diamonds and a long black hood."[24]

For English colonists in Connecticut, no such touch was possible. So when Cotton Mather reported a homegrown cure, its ingredients were carefully selected for both their medical and symbolic properties. He advised sufferers to seek out, "a thistle call'd the *Boar-Thistle*; very short and prickly," and make a "decoction" of it with "*Cancer Root*, and a sort of *Devils Bit*." He assured his London correspondents that the plant, "is a Cure for the *King's-Evil*, tho' very far gone," and the roots could be directly applied to the swollen lymph nodes for additional relief.[25]

If Mather was himself dismissive of the healing powers of the royal touch, the potent symbolism of his medicinal substitute is clear. New Englanders could not present themselves in London for the Queen's healing touch, but the hardy thistles sprouting from rocky fields nearby could serve the same function in her absence. It seems that the thistles painted on these chests could serve a related function. Although a great distance—in culture, religion, politics, and geography—separated London from the Connecticut shore, these painted chests served as daily reminders of the monarch.

Returning to the question that began this section, why did thistles, crowns, *fleurs-de-lis*, roses, tulips, and birds appeal to Connecticut colonists in the early-eighteenth century? The historical associations of these different symbols offer important insight into the meanings hiding in plain sight on the surfaces of these chests. The thistles, roses, crowns, and *fleurs-de-lis* painted on these chests reference well known political iconography that survives to the present day. Yet to Connecticut eyes in the early eighteenth-century, the many meanings they carried were complicated. Painted on a piece of household furniture, a common weed like a thistle could indicate a new sense of *Britishness* when placed alongside concentric roses and *fleurs-de-lis*. If each of these symbols represented individual kingdoms in the past, their combined gestalt indicated the recent emergence of Great Britain from its constituent parts.

Like Samuel Sewall in Boston writing to a London merchant to seek guidance about the latest fashions, consumers in coastal Connecticut worked to stay abreast of new developments in politics and style. Painted beautifully with rich colors, the decoration on these chests appealed to tastes for natural imagery while also suggesting a wide range of meaningful associations. It might remind a viewer of powers associated with the monarch in England who was charged with protecting royal subjects at home and abroad. It could also recall traditional folk beliefs and superstitions. The painting on these chests is not remarkable for any one of these associations on its own, but rather in its ability to reference a broad range of meanings with a set of simple, beautiful, and humble images.

In the years that followed this flourishing of painted furniture in Saybrook and Guilford, Connecticut craftsmen in other towns continued to develop vibrant decoration for fashionable forms. In Windsor from the 1730s to 1750s, a practice emerged for ornamental painting with novel emulation of earlier Japanning. In architectural woodwork, shop signs, military insignia, and other decorated surfaces, ornamental painters used bold colors and refined technique to elevate humble surfaces with evocative compositions. As new information about these related practices comes to light in the future, scholars may uncover new connections to the chests made along the Connecticut shore.

Those painted chests from Saybrook and Guilford present a peculiar paradox in the story of American furniture. They appeared during a period when English colonists in New England began to cultivate an independent identity, bolstered by icons of resistance like the Charter Oak at Hartford. Scholars have characterized their parallels in American furniture—like the carved Hadley-type chests of an earlier generation to the north—as having a unique spirit suggestive of a growing distance between English and American styles. Yet the Saybrook or Guilford chests paint a more complicated picture of Connecticut politics in the early years of the eighteenth century. If some colonists embraced a new American identity, others embraced the signs, symbols, and trappings of the British Empire as seen on these chests.

That this type of painting does not appear on furniture in England or Scotland is a testament to the complicated processes that brought fashions and tastes from English shops to New England homes. The craftsmen who made these chests and the consumers who purchased them wanted fashionable goods in the latest styles. They also wanted objects that reflected their identity as modern British citizens. Using bold colors to paint images of imperial power and unity, they created a distinctive tradition to achieve both ends.

NOTES

1 Patricia Kane, *Furniture of the New Haven Colony: The Seventeenth Century* (New Haven: The New Haven Colony Historical Society, 1973), 55.

2 Kevin M. Sweeney, "Mansion People: Kinship, Class, and Architecture in Western Massachusetts in the Mid Eighteenth Century," *Winterthur Portfolio* 19:4 (Winter 1984), 243.

3 R.O.M. Carter and H.M. Carter, "The Foliate Head in England," *Folklore* 78:4 (Winter 1967), 269–274.

4 Gilman C. Gates, *Saybrook at the Mouth of the Connecticut* (Orange, CT: Press of the W.H. Lee Co., 1935), 182.

5 Robert F. Trent, "A Channel Islands Parallel for the Early Eighteenth Century Connecticut Chests Attributed to Charles Guillam," *Studies in the Decorative Arts* 2:1 (Fall 1994), 81–82.

6 Jessica Arista and Dr. Jennifer Mass, *Technical Study of a Painted High Chest from Saybrook, Connecticut (1710–1727) in the Henry Francis du Pont Winterthur Museum,* 2009. Conservation File for High Chest 1957.1110, H.F. du Pont's Winterthur Museum, Garden, and Library.

7 Frances Gruber Safford, *American Furniture In The Metropolitan Museum of Art: I. Early Colonial Period, The Seventeenth-Century and William and Mary Styles* (New York: The Metropolitan Museum of Art, 2007), 259–260.

8 Erwin Panofsky, "What is Baroque?" in Panofsky, *Three Essays on Style* (Cambridge, MA: The Massachusetts Institute of Technology Press, 1995), 20–25.

9 Waldron Belknap, Jr. *American Colonial Painting: Materials for a History* (Cambridge, MA: Belknap Press of the Harvard University Press, 1959), 273–300.

10 William I. Roberts, III, "Samuel Storke: An Eighteenth-Century London Merchant Trading to the American Colonies," *The Business History Review* 39: 2 (Summer 1965), 147–150.

11 Cynthia A. Kierner, *Traders and Gentlefolk: The Livingstons of New York, 1675–1790* (Ithaca: The Cornell University Press, 1992), 69.

12 Samuel Sewall letter to Samuel Storke, February 20, 1720. As printed in *Letter-Book of Samuel Sewall* (Boston: The Massachusetts Historical Society, 1888), 105–107.

13 Gerald W.R. Ward, *American Case Furniture in the Mabel Brady Garvan and Other Collections at Yale University* (New Haven: Yale University Art Gallery, 1988), 95–100.

14 Safford, *American Furniture In The Metropolitan Museum of Art: I*, 219–220

15 Safford, *American Furniture In The Metropolitan Museum of Art: I*, 249–250.

16 Malcolm A. Norton, "Chests of Our New England Grandmothers," *The Magazine Antiques* II: 2 (August 1922), 77–78.

17 While the precise volume that introduced this decorative printed motif to Saybrook and Guilford is unknown, it was actively used in the bustling shop of the seventeenth-century London printer John Macock. Macock had three presses that produced widely disseminated political, scientific, historical, and theological texts. The New England Company, an evangelical group formed in 1649 "for the propagation of the Gospel in New England" commissioned printings from his shop

18 Trent, "A Channel Islands Parallel," 77. Dean A. Fales, Jr. *American Painted Furniture 1660–1880* (New York: Bonanza Books, 1986), 25–29.

19 William Salmon, *Botanologia: The English Herbal, or History of Plants* (London: Printed by I. Dawks, 1710), 1137–1151.

20 Salmon, *Botanologia*, 1136

21 Salmon, *Botanologia*, 1148

22 Salmon, *Botanologia*, 1136

23 Hugh Clark, *A Concise History of Knighthood* (London: Printed for W. Straham et al., 1784), 126–141. http://books.google.com.

24 Raymond Crawfurd, *The King's Evil* (Oxford: The Clarendon Press, 1911), 143–145. http://books.google.com.

25 Cotton Mather, "An Extract of Several Letters from Cotton Mather, D.D. to John Woodward, M.D. and Richard Waller, Esq," *Philosophical Transactions* 29 (1714–1716), 64. http://www.jstor.org/stable/103038.

USE

Chests in many forms—with drawers, of drawers, on stands, on feet, painted, plain, large, and small—were common features of colonial New England homes. Produced in great volume and sold at an inexpensive price, a wooden chest could serve any number of functions. In a modest household with limited resources and a small suite of domestic furnishings, a locking chest might be the only secure space for the storage of textiles, documents, or personal valuables. In a wealthy household with a great volume of case furniture and imported luxuries, a wooden chest could be found in the kitchen or garret for the storage of useful supplies. The specific domestic context of a chest greatly shaped its different functions and uses.

Several patterns emerge in domestic inventories from the Connecticut shore in the early eighteenth century. If a household had one chest, it was likely to have had several of different qualities. Probate inventories are filled with references to old chests, new chests, meal chests, chests with locks, and chests missing lids among many varieties. Used for storage in a time when homes were relatively porous spaces occupied by extended families and communities, the ability secure valuables in a piece of locked furniture was important for domestic organization and order.

In Saybrook and Guilford in the eighteenth century, these chests were both beautiful additions to careful domestic assemblages, and important tools used to organize and order the home.

UNDER LOCK AND KEY In his 1731 *Directions to Servants*, the Irish satirist Jonathan Swift (1667–1745) pilloried the behaviors and misbehaviors of English domestic culture. In the chapter "Directions to the Waiting Maid," he warns the titular servant that, "two accidents have happened to lessen the Comforts and profits of your Employment." The first was the "execrable Custom got among Ladies" of reusing the expensive silks of their dresses when they fell out of fashion, where earlier habits dictated that old clothing be given to maids. Instead of gifting them to the waiting maid, they began, "trucking their old Cloaths for *China*," "turning them to cover easy Chairs," and "turning them into patch-work for Screens, Stools, Cushions, and the like." The second accident was, "the Invention of small Chests

1 *Tea Canister*, 1685-1717. Painted by Marmaduck Cradock (born 1655), London, England. Painted metal. H: 6 1/4 in. W: 9 1/2 in. D: 5 1/3 in. Victoria and Albert Museum, London, UK, Given by Thomas Sutton, Esq., in memory of his wife, W.70-1919.

and Trunks, with Lock and Key," where a wealthy woman could control access to sugar and tea, or other domestic valuables to which maids were often suspected of helping themselves (Fig. 1).[1]

Although Swift's concern in this work is primarily humor, he outlines important tensions concerning privacy, access, and security in eighteenth-century homes. Objects like the Saybrook or Guilford painted chests were made in part to mediate those tensions, allowing the holder of the key to control access to certain spaces in a home that was otherwise open. A house in this period might include several generations of a single family, domestic servants, enslaved Africans, apprentices, and others who populated the greater household. Many members of the community might have access to the home in different social or official capacities. Expensive goods had a habit of disappearing.

S. view of the Hempstead House, New London.

Rather than merely holding valuable goods, locking chests like those made in Saybrook and Guilford were used to secure them. Modern antiquarians have celebrated these chests for their distinctive painting, but their most important functional features for day-to-day use in the eighteenth century were their large locks. Swift satirized the pretenses of the British middle class in his *Directions to Servants*, and members of that same class making the same missteps populated the prominent households of the colonial Connecticut shore.

Joshua Hempstead of nearby New London (1678–1758) kept a diary for 47 years, and the extensive surviving pages provide the most complete textual account of daily life in coastal Connecticut in the early eighteenth century (Fig. 2). On Saturday, May 3, 1746, he recorded the events of a frustrating day; after he "mended fence in Crossman Lot & pickt up Stones in Gilbert Lower lot," he noted, "Lost my keys 3 tyed with a Leather String. How they got out of my pocket I cannot Conceive. I had them at home at Dinner time. My Cheast Desk & Drawers key." Unable to find the keys, he was forced to dismantle his chest, desk, and chest of drawers to access their contents. On Monday, May 5, he wrote, "I was at home most of the day taking of my Cheast Lock & breaking open my Desk &c."[2]

While working in the field, Hempstead lost his keys. This minor episode describes a mundane frustration today that carried meaningful ramifications in the period. If he could not open the locks to his chest, desk, and chest of drawers, anyone who found the keys would be able to do so and make away with his property.

As a local magistrate, Hempstead was well aware of how common domestic theft was in eighteenth-century Connecticut. On March 30, 1727, he recorded in his diary that Irish immigrant William Watkins was, "Branded in ye forehead & had

2 John Warner Barber (1798–1885), *S. View of the Hempstead House, New London*, 1836. As printed in Barber's *Connecticut Historical Collections* (New Haven, Printed by B.L. Hamlen, 1836), 287.

his Right Ear Cut of" after being convicted of "breaking into Mr Chapmans house on the Sabath or lords day & Stealing a hatt Cloth's & money to ye value of £22."[3] On August 14, 1728, Richard Jacobs was brought to court "on Suspicion of Stealing 5 gall Rum." On August 21 of the same year, Richard Beebee, Jonathan Hamilton, Thankful Harris, and Mary Hamilton were brought to court "on Suspicion of Stealing Watermelions" from Jonathan Boles.[4] On May 11, 1736, he examined the trial of "Jenny Negro Woman of Mr. Treats Concerning Stealing Mr Dureys wine," a trial that continued on May 14. On May 24 of the same year, he held Court at the town prison for the trial about "Appleby Stealing a £3 bill from Lampson & Cloths from Wickham."[5] Although the punishments for thieves could be severe, the crime's continued appearances in these and many other episodes in Hempstead's diary suggests its banality. Small goods disappeared with great frequency from the home. Sometimes a suspect was apprehended, but more often than not the crime went unsolved.

On November 30, 1753, Joshua Hempstead recorded some dismaying news after spending the previous night visiting the home of his friend Captain Joseph Coit. While he was away his grandchildren Grover and William and their friend Joshua Starr "kindled a fire & Roasted Potatoes & played a while in my Room." When he returned, he found, "I lost my old Silver Spoon markt I.A.H it Lay with one more not markt on the Cupboard," and suspected that the boys were responsible for its disappearance: "I Supose they all Combined to hide the Spoon or Else worse."[6]

This brief passage reveals a number of important details about life in Hempstead's home. It records that the home was used by at least three generations of the Hempstead family, and they shared access to different rooms. The wider community—like Joshua Starr, friend of the diarist's grandchildren—found its way into even private chambers. If certain rules applied when Joshua was home, they were disregarded when he was away. Most importantly, when valuables were left "on the Cupboard" and not locked inside, they quickly went missing.

With this context in mind, it is easy to see why the loss of three keys was so distressing for Joshua Hempstead. Theft was common, and many different people had ready access to his home. To keep valuable goods and important documents safe, he locked them in his chest, desk, or chest of drawers.

The painted chests from Saybrook and Guilford were made to serve a similar purpose. Sealed with a lock, they allowed the key holder to secure and protect important property.

DOMESTIC ASSEMBLAGES The painted chests from Saybrook and Guilford were made as part of complex domestic ensembles. Residing in Connecticut homes alongside textiles, metal wares, glass, ceramics, engraved prints, and paintings, they were one part of a space rich with visual and tactile stimulation. Only two examples survive with histories of ownership in the eighteenth century, but these two help illuminate the broader material contexts for which these chests were made.

Where histories are known, the chests are associated with both middling and prominent families of comfortable means. They would have been used alongside luxuries like Joshua Hempstead's silver spoon, and utilitarian goods made of pewter, earthenware, or cotton.

Now in the collections of the Henry Whitfield State Museum in Guilford, a modestly painted 1710–1730 chest has an oral history of eighteenth-century ownership in the Hand family of Guilford, and Munger family of East Guilford, modern Madison (Figs. 3 & 4). According to family tradition, Captain Daniel Hand (1732–1816) of Guilford gifted this chest to his daughter Esther Hand Munger (1760–1846) when she married and moved to East Guilford. It ultimately passed to Esther's distant nephew Wilbur Pardee (1861–1932) who gifted it to the museum.[7] Like other chests of the early-eighteenth century, the Hand/Munger family chest combines old-fashioned joinery with up-to-date decoration. The painting combines large images like the birds painted on either side with smaller floral motifs painted across the front of the chest attached to scrolling vines. Given the date of manufacture for a chest of this type and Daniel Hand's date of birth, he was likely the second owner of the chest. The original owner is not identified, but it may have been one of Daniel's parents, Jannah Hand (1693–1767) or Dorothy Griswold (1693–1773) of Guilford.

Although family tradition has it that Esther Munger inherited this chest from her father upon her marriage—complete with tales of Esther riding side-saddle on a horse to her new home, followed by her brother carrying the chest with her trousseau—this story may have gathered embellishment in the retelling. If instead it descended to Esther after her father's death, then it may be one of the chests listed in Daniel Hand's 1817 estate inventory.

Hand's inventory includes a long list of wooden furniture. He owned a desk ($5.00), stand table ($3.00), oval table ($2.00), two maple tables ($.75 and $1.00, respectively), two candlestands ($.50 and $.75), case of drawers ($5.00), great chair ($.50), 6 brown chairs ($6.00), 4 fiddleback chairs ($2.40), and 2 broken chairs ($1.00). He owned a linen chest ($2.00), old trunk ($.50), small chest with lock and key ($.50), and a chest with one drawer ($2.00). Most significantly, his inventory includes, "flower'd chest with drawers 3.0 chest do. 6.0 low flower'd chest 1.25 red linen chest 2.0."[8]

Even though the Hand/Munger chest would have been nearly 100 years old in 1817, Daniel Hand's inventory presents two plausible entries for the chest here illustrated. Certainly the ground color on the chest appears red today, so the red chest valued at $2.00 may refer to this piece. Alternatively, the three "flower'd" chests listed—chest with drawers, chest, and low chest—may have included this

3 *Chest with Drawer*, 1710–1730. Made in Guilford, CT. Oak, pine, tulip poplar; paint. H: 32 5/6 in. W: 45 1/4 in. D: 20 1/4 in. Henry Whitfield State Museum, Guilford, CT. Gift of Mr. Wilbur Pardee, 59.1919.

4 *Chest with Drawer* (front panel detail), Henry Whitfield State Museum, Guilford, CT. Gift of Mr. Wilbur Pardee, 59.1919.

piece, and indicate that it was parts of a larger suite of related furniture when it was made. The latter fact would help explain the formal variety seen in the surviving chests that include small boxes, chests of drawers, high chests, and a chest on stand by illustrating that these pieces were potentially made as part of larger suites that have not survived intact.

The adjective "flower'd" appears elsewhere in Hand's inventory, and seems to refer generally to surfaces with vegetal ornamentation. His textiles included a flower'd tan coverlet valued $3.50, and a flower'd blue and white coverlet valued $1.50. His tablewares included 4 flower'd china plates valued $.66, and two blue flower'd china plates valued $.10. These most likely refer to very different types of ornamentation—stitched, woven, or quilted flowers on the coverlets, and underglaze painting on the porcelain—in very different flowered motifs.

Used to differentiate one piece from another of the same form in the long inventory list, flower'd denotes a general type of decoration relative to other examples of the same form identified by a single color.[9] This adjective applied to furniture, imported ceramics, and also would have applied to textiles like this needlework bed hanging from Wethersfield, Connecticut, stitched with the same thistles, tulips, roses, and vines painted on the Saybrook and Guilford chests. (Fig. 5)

5 *Bed Curtain* detail, ca. 1745, embroidered by Sarah Noyes Chester (1722-1797), Wethersfield, CT. Linen embroidered with wool. H: 87 3/4 in. W: 70 5/8 in. Metropolitan Museum of Art, New York, Gift of Mr. and Mrs. Frank Coit Johnson, through their son and daughter, 1944.140.

6 *Chair*, 1649. Made in England. Beech; knotted wool upholstery. H: 32 3/4 in. W: 18 1/4 in. D: 15 1/4 in. Victoria and Albert Museum, London, UK, 428–1896.

Like many middling rural New Englanders, Daniel Hand owned a mix of utilitarian and luxurious objects, new furniture and older pieces. His tablewares included a silver porringer, spoons, and pepper caster used alongside pewter plates and platters. His ceramics included the porcelain discussed above as well as stoneware and earthenware used alongside it. His home was a visually rich assemblage of objects with pink glass bottles, striped calico quilts, plaid blankets, white cotton, and brass kettles. A polychrome painted chest like this example would have fit right in.

Flower'd objects also appear earlier in eighteenth-century inventories from Saybrook and Guilford homes, offering enticing clues about the original context for the style.

Following Nathaniel Lynde's (1659–1729) death in Saybrook, his estate inventory recorded a remarkable level of wealth and luxury that was otherwise unknown in the region. Lynde was an early treasurer of the Collegiate School that became Yale College, and donated a building and land to the young school to settle it in Saybrook. With a total value of £8,305:3:4, his estate included an extensive list of furniture, textiles, metalwares, ceramics, and other household furnishings. Lynde's estate includes four enslaved Africans named Cesar, Juba, Nero, and Rose. He owned two great chairs and "leathern" chairs, eight "Turkey work'd chairs," six "new chairs," a "high cubbard," "red cedar table," and a "long settle." His silver included a 30 ½ oz. tankard, a 17 oz. sugar box, a 30 oz. salt cellar, and a 30 oz. dish. Other luxuries included two cups made of coconut shells with silver rims and feet, a tortoise shell box with silver fittings, a piece of coral set in gold, a pearl necklace, a diamond locket, "Queen Elizabeth's Cup," several embroidered pictures, and a map of London. He also owned a small silver "flowered box."[10] Lynde's domestic luxuries have not survived to the present day, but contemporaneous examples of several distinctive forms are illustrated in figures 6 and 7.

Three local men, Thomas Buckingham, William Tully, and Daniel Buckingham took Nathaniel Lynde's inventory. As discussed in the first chapter, Daniel Buckingham was a Saybrook joiner who lived adjacent to Charles Guillam, and is considered a possible maker of the painted chests.

One remarkable chest is thought to have been owned by William Tully (1676–1744), who left a valuable estate worth £3301:8:5 when he died in 1744. Although modest in comparison to Lynde's estate, it included multiple suits of clothing, six bedsteads with feather mattresses, bolsters, blankets, and sheets, more than a dozen books of theology, a 27 oz. silver tankard, and in the West Chamber of his house, "one Trunk with 2 Draws" and a "Large Chest." His inventory was taken by Samuel Doty, Joshua Bushnell, and Nathaniel Lynde, Jr. (1672–1768).[11]

7 *Standing Salt*, ca. 1700. Made by John Edwards (ca. 1671–1746), Boston, Massachusetts. Silver. H: 7 7/8 in. Diam: 5 7/16 in. Weight: 12 oz. 18 dwt. Metropolitan Museum of Art, New York, Gift of Sarah Hayward Draper, 1972. 1972.204.

8 *Chest*, ca. 1710–1730. Made in Saybrook, CT. Pine, oak, tulip poplar; paint. H: 22 in. W: 44 1/4 in. D: 20 1/4. Old Saybrook Historical Society.

9 *Chest* (right side detail), ca. 1710–1730. Old Saybrook Historical Society.

10 *Chest* (left side detail), ca. 1710–1730. Old Saybrook Historical Society.

11 *Chest* (back detail), ca. 1710–1730. Old Saybrook Historical Society.

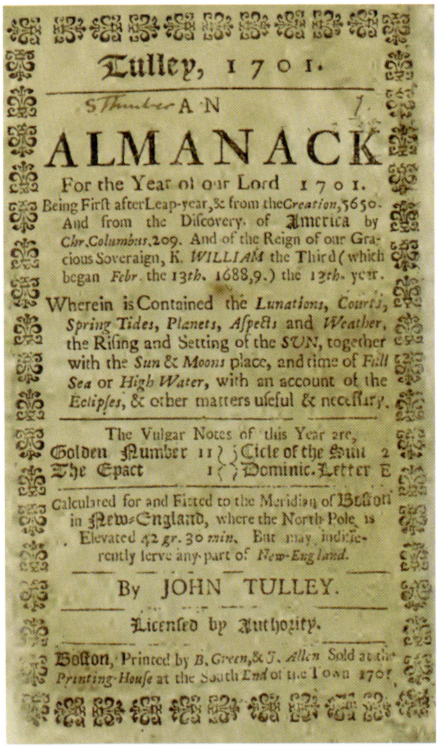
Tulley, 1701.

AN

ALMANACK

For the Year of our Lord 1701.

Being First after Leap-year, & from the Creation, 5650. And from the Discovery of America by Chr. Columbus, 209. And of the Reign of our Gracious Soveraign, K. WILLIAM the Third (which began Febr. the 13th. 1688,9.) the 13th. year.

Wherein is Contained the Lunations, Courts, Spring Tides, Planets, Aspects and Weather, the Rising and Setting of the SUN, together with the Sun & Moons place, and time of Full Sea or High Water, with an account of the Eclipses, & other matters useful & necessary.

The Vulgar Notes of this Year are,

Golden Number 11 | Circle of the Sun 2

The Epact 1 | Dominic. Letter E

Calculated for and Fitted to the Meridian of Boston in New-England, where the North Pole is Elevated 42 gr. 30 min. But may indifferently serve any part of New-England.

By JOHN TULLEY.

Licensed by Authority.

Boston, Printed by B. Green, & J. Allen. Sold at the Printing-House at the South End of the Town 1701.

12 Title page of John Tully's 1701 *Almanack* (Boston: Printed by B. Green and J. Allen).

In 1880 Dr. William Tully (1809–1880) of Old Saybrook, the twice-great-grandson of Nathaniel Lynde's neighbor of the same name, willed that chest filled with books, document, and other historical curiosities to the Acton Public Library in Old Saybrook, which then also served as a museum of local history (Figs. 8–11).[12]

William Tully was a prominent citizen of Saybrook. His father John Tully (1626–1701) was an early settler of the town, and published a yearly almanac for New England from 1682 until his death (Fig. 12).[13] As evidenced by his inventory of Nathaniel Lynde's luxurious estate, Tully was familiar with the fashionable tastes of the day. His own wealth filled his home with a volume of textiles, silver, and furniture that was rare in colonial coastal Connecticut.

Tully commissioned this *flowered* chest in keeping with the material and visual richness of that domestic assemblage. It was made locally of inexpensive woods with simple joinery, but its bold painting in bright colors made it a suitable companion for the imported luxuries Tully kept in his home. Just as his friend Nathaniel Lynde kept a map of London and "Queen Elizabeth's Cup" alongside his extensive holdings of silver, furniture, textiles, and books, William Tully commissioned objects of local manufacture that expressed his local prominence as a British colonist.

Nathaniel Lynde owned a small flowered box of silver. William Tully commissioned a boldly polychrome painted flowered chest.

NOTES

1 Jonathan Swift, *Directions to Servants* (Dublin: Printed by George Faulker, 1741), 63–64.

2 Joshua Hempstead, *Diary of Joshua Hempstead* (New London: The New London County Historical Society, 1901), 459.

3 Hempstead, *Diary*, 182.

4 Hempstead, *Diary*, 201.

5 Hempstead, *Diary*, 303.

6 Hempstead, *Diary*, 619-620.

7 Henry Whitfield State Museum curatorial files, 59.1919. Guilford, CT.

8 Captain Daniel Hand estate inventory, January 20, 1817. Guilford Probate vol. 19, 204–205.

9 Robert F. Trent, "A Channel Islands Parallel for the Early Eighteenth-Century Connecticut Chests Attributed to Charles Guillam," *Studies in the Decorative Arts* 2:1 (Fall 1994), 81

10 Nathaniel Lynde estate inventory, April 3, 1730. Guilford Probate vol. 2, 361–371.

11 William Tully estate inventory, September 4, 1744. Guilford Probate vol. 4, 249–254.

12 Harriet Chapman Chesebrough, *Glimpses of Saybrook in Colonial Days* (Old Saybrook: Published by Celebration 3½ to Commemorate the 350th Anniversary of the Saybrook Colony, 1985), 42–43.

13 Charles Barney Whittelsey, *Genealogy of the Whittelsey-Whittlesey Family* (Hartford: Press of the Case, Lockwood, and Brainard Company, 1898), 61.

H
V

HISTORY

The journey that brought the painted chests of Saybrook and Guilford from Connecticut homes to museum galleries charts a complex transition from useful object to icon of vernacular design. As discussed in the previous chapter, these chests served a specific domestic purpose when new. Owners used them to store and secure household valuables from prying eyes and unscrupulous hands. Some of these chests remained in active use for several generations. As tastes and styles changed, the once fashionable objects were likely relegated to back rooms, attics, porches, and barns where they sat in dusty obscurity.

In the late nineteenth century as the United States became an increasingly industrial, multicultural, and urban nation, an interest developed in the early history of colonial America. Now called the "Colonial Revival," this period saw Americans look back into their history to rediscover the stories, people, and culture of the past. Reacting against the perceived excesses of Victorian taste, this Colonial Revival sparked a growing interest in historic American architecture and decorative arts.

It was against this backdrop that these painted chests first came to light to a new generation of scholars and collectors. Few in number, diverse in form, and eccentric in ornament, they presented a challenge to the linear thinking that characterized early studies of American decorative arts. That initial confusion—over the age of these pieces, the origin of their painting, and their possible maker—lingered for many years, and hindered subsequent scholars of this material.

1 *Chest-on-Frame*, 1705–1725. Made in Saybrook or Guilford, CT. Yellow poplar, chestnut, birch, ash, oak, white cedar; paint. H: 37 in. W: 30 1/4 in. D: 19 1/2 in. Metropolitan Museum of Art, New York, Gift of Mrs. Russell Sage, 1909. 10.125.15.

2 *Chest with Drawer*, 1705–1725. Made in Saybrook or Guilford, CT. Yellow poplar, yellow pine, birch; paint. H: 19 1/2 in. W: 29 1/2 in. D: 16 1/2 in. Metropolitan Museum of Art, New York. Gift of Mrs. Russell Sage, 1909. 10.125.16

EARLY COLLECTORS When pioneering early collectors began to explore the story of American furniture in the late nineteenth century, they began by searching for regional, stylistic, and chronological progressions. It was generally believed in the nineteenth century that the old chests found in New England had been brought from England by the earliest colonists. At that time the Hand/Munger family chest discussed in the previous chapter was thought to have come from England in the seventeenth century.[1]

Irving W. Lyon's (1840–1896) *The Colonial Furniture of New England* (1891) was one of the earliest published studies of American furniture. A doctor in Hartford, Connecticut, Lyon based his study on his examination of antique furniture he encountered in the region around that city. When Lyon began his examination of colonial furniture, little was known about joiners of that period. By documenting many examples of the carved sunflower-type chests discussed elsewhere in this catalogue in the towns surrounding Hartford, he persuasively argued to his peers that the geographical specificity of their distribution and their shared formal characteristics suggested a Connecticut origin in the area.[2]

THE BEST TWELVE COUNTRY HOUSES IN AMERICA
BY HENRY H SAYLOR
IX
WESTOMERE THE HOME OF GEORGE S PALMER ESQ
AT NEW LONDON, CONN.
Charles A Platt Architect

IN MY quest for the best in American country house architecture, last spring I visited the James River country in Virginia. Together with the romances of Thomas Nelson Page—those priceless records of a South that was and is no more—there had been associated in my mind the famous James River mansions. There is Shirley, the home of the Carters since 1723; Brandon, established by Nathanial Harrison about 1700; Carter's Grove, built in 1746 by Carter Burwell; and there we find Westover, the home of the "genial seigneur," Colonel William Byrd, 2d, who at his death left this magnificent estate of 179,440 acres and upon it the finest mansion of Virginia. Twice ravaged by Benedict Arnold, viciously attacked by Cornwallis, used as a camping ground by McClellan, trampled by Fitz-John Porter's lawless troops, who stabled their horses in the church, it is great wonder that anything of Westover remains. Yet it still stands, its pineapple decoration—symbol of hospitality—intact; and Mrs. Ramsay, a collateral descendant of "William the Great of Westover" is bringing it back to much of its former splendor.

Surely, here among these glorious homes of the young South should be found some of the best country houses that America has to show. Yet I left the James River country with sadness in my heart, for its glory had passed away. The river highway long ago gave place to the railroad, and it in turn sought more thickly populated lands, leaving in a backwater of civilization's path this glorious countryside.

The houses that have appeared previously in this series are those of:

I. MR. JAMES L. BREESE, SOUTHAMPTON, L. I.
II. MR. JOHN T. PRATT, GLEN COVE, L. I.
III. MR. CHARLES Z. KLAUDER, MT. AIRY, PA.
IV. MR. ELECTUS D. LITCHFIELD, NEW CANAAN, CONN.
V. MR. JOHN W. PEPPER, JENKINTOWN, PA.
VI. MR. J. WALDRON GILLESPIE, MONTECITO, CAL.
VII. MR. FRANCIS T. UNDERHILL, SANTA BARBARA, CAL.
VIII. MR. TRUMAN H. NEWBERRY, GROSSE POINTE FARMS, MICH.

Westomere from the southeastern corner, showing the front that looks out upon the Thames River, just as Westover in Virginia looks out upon the James
26

By using careful analysis and logical examination, Lyon helped shape early thought about American furniture. Some of his thinking proved prescient. In his examination of regional contexts, Lyon shepherded in the notion that different locations produced distinctive traditions of furniture.

Lyon was part of a small group of dedicated furniture collectors in Hartford that included upholsterer Walter Hosmer (1830–1911). Hosmer owned at least two of the painted Saybrook or Guilford chests; a chest-on-stand and a small, meticulously painted chest-with-drawer (Figs. 1 & 2). In 1894 Hosmer sold his collection to the cousins George S. Palmer (1855–1934) and H. Eugene Bolles (1853–1910). Palmer was a New London industrialist who collected American and English art. His New London home Westomere was designed as a replica of Westover, the Georgian plantation home built ca. 1750 for the Byrd family of Virginia. The house was named one of "The Best Twelve Country Houses in America" by *Country Life in America* magazine in 1916 (Fig. 3). Bolles was a Waterford-born lawyer working in Dorchester, Massachusetts.[3]

With romantic visions of the preindustrial past shaped by the Colonial Revival, Palmer and Bolles were wealthy men who collected American furniture for both aesthetic and patriotic reasons. Palmer was particularly known for his mid-eighteenth-century furniture from Boston, Newport, and Philadelphia, and began first by collecting English antiques before deciding, as author Henry H. Saylor paraphrased, "we had craftsmen in our own land that could hold their own with their better known English contemporaries."[4]

3 In 1916, George S. Palmer's colonial revivial country home Westomere, designed by Charles A. Platt, was named one of, "The Best Twelve Country Houses In America," by *Country Life in America* 29:3 (January 1916), 26–29.

4 *Chest*, 1715–1730. Made in Saybrook or Guilford, CT. Oak, chestnut, tulip poplar; paint. H: 34 ½ in. W: 47 ½ in. D: 20 in. From the Collection of The Henry Ford, Dearborn, MI, 36.141.2.

5 *Chest* (front panel detail), 1717–1730. From the Collection of The Henry Ford, Dearborn, MI, 36.141.2.

Bolles, whose collection included important examples of seventeenth-century American furniture, took ownership of the two painted Saybrook or Guilford chests. In 1909 they were gifted to The Metropolitan Museum of Art when the philanthropist Mrs. Olivia Sage (1828–1918), purchased Bolles' collection for the museum.[5]

These chests were dubbed "Guilford Chests" at the time because by tradition curator Joseph Downs had uncovered a related chest of drawers in East Guilford.[6] When Malcolm A. Norton published a brief article titled "Chests of Our New England Grandmothers" in *The Magazine Antiques* in 1922, he compared the "Guilford Chests" to the more numerous surviving "Hadley Chests" and "Sunflower Chests" as distinctive New England regional traditions. By that time a patriotic zeal for American craftsmanship had replaced the earlier notion of a European origin for early American chests. Norton observed, "to a collector of American antiques an English or foreign-made chest offers little of interest."[7]

Norton looked to the iconography of a chest now in the collections of The Henry Ford (Figs. 4 & 5) to date this group erroneously to the middle-seventeenth century. Along with the Hadley and Sunflower chests, he considered the Guilford

6 Martin Partyka (1907–1954), *Guilford Painted Chest*, ca. 1936. Watercolor, gouache, and ink on paper. H: 9 5/8 in. W: 13 9/16 in. Index of American Design, National Gallery of Art, Washington, D.C., 1943.8.4676.

7 Martin Partyka (1907–1954), *Guilford Painted Chest*, ca. 1936. Watercolor, colored pencil, gouache, and graphite on paperboard. H: 11 in. W: 11 7/16 in. Index of American Design, National Gallery of Art, Washington, D.C., 1943.8.4675.

8 Martin Partyka (1907–1954), *Guilford Painted Chest*, ca. 1936. Watercolor, colored pencil, gouache, and graphite on paperboard. H: 11 3/8 in. W: 9 9/16 in. Index of American Design, National Gallery of Art, Washington, D.C., 1943.8.4677.

pieces to be a "major classification" of New England's seventeenth-century chests.[8] The noted antiquarian Wallace Nutting followed this lead, identifying a region around the Connecticut coast as the place of origin for this tradition in 1924 when he updated his *Furniture of the Pilgrim Century*.[9]

The Guilford origin for these chests was generally accepted until the 1930s. In 1935 historian Gilman C. Gates published *Saybrook at the Mouth of the Connecticut: The First One Hundred Years* to mine the local stories of Saybrook in the early colonial period. He included a rough transcription of Charles Guillam's 1727 probate inventory as evidence of his profession along with several historical documents relating to the Guillam family.[10] Gates was not a furniture historian, and seems to have been drawn to Guillam's inventory for its unusual level of detail for a woodworker.

The tantalizing details of this inventory were quickly connected with the well-known and increasingly rare "Guilford Chests" eagerly sought by prominent collectors, transforming them into "Saybrook Chests." The inventory was already known by 1932 when the Hartford antiques dealer William B. Goodwin cited details seemingly drawn from it in a letter to the collector Henry Francis du Pont as proof that Guillam was the cabinetmaker of a diminutive chest and a high chest Goodwin had for sale.[11] Both the high chest, illustrated in chapter one (pg. 7), and the diminutive chest were sold to du Pont and became part of his renowned collections of American decorative arts.

Despite the then-recent recent reattribution to Saybrook, three chests were identified with Guilford in 1936 when artists working for the Index of American Design painted them as part of that monumental effort to document the history of American material culture and folk art. The Index, which operated from 1935

to 1942 and grew to include over 18,000 watercolor paintings, was organized under the Federal Art Project of the Works Progress Administration during the Great Depression. The Index was conceived by textile designer Ruth Reeves (1892–1966) and Romana Javitz (1903–1980) of the New York Public Library's Picture Collection. The Index was formed to record the precise details of American historical material culture with the goal of educating the general public as well as designers, and preserving history at risk of being lost.[12]

The seven paintings show three different chests from different angles. Martin Partyka produced three views the chest of drawers now at the Wadsworth Atheneum (Figs. 6–8). Edward F. Engel painted two views of the chest then at the Acton

9 Edward F. Engel (1887–1978), *Painted Guilford Chest*, 1935/1942. Watercolor, colored pencil, ink, and graphite on paper. H: 9 5/8 in. W: 16 1/4 in. Index of American Design, National Gallery of Art, Washington, D.C., 1943.8.4629.

10 Edward F. Engel (1887–1978), *Painted Guilford Chest*, 1935/1942. Watercolor, colored pencil, gouache, and graphite on paperboard. H: 14 9/16 in. W: 21 7/8 in. Index of American Design, National Gallery of Art, Washington, D.C., 1943.8.4634.

Public Library in Old Saybrook, now at the Old Saybrook Historical Society (Fig. 9–10). Isabella Ruth Doerfler created two views of a polychrome painted chest that is certainly not part of the same group, but illustrates the qualities then erroneously associated with the Saybrook or Guilford chests (Fig. 11–12).

These precisely limned works highlight a shift in the way Americans engaged with objects from the past. While earlier scholars and collectors wrote about American historic furniture as a link to historic people and events—such as Malcolm Norton's chests "Of Our New England Grandmothers"—the Index of American Design celebrated formal qualities of antique furniture for its ability to inform the thinking of modern designers.

In 1957, two events marked yet another important shift in scholarship of Saybrook or Guilford painted chests. What had once been the province of wealthy collectors and antiques dealers expanded to include the academic examination of the same materials. Inspired by its foundation in the study of art history, many scholars of this period worked to connect surviving furniture to identified furniture makers. That year marked the publication of Ethel Hall Bjerkoe's landmark *The Cabinetmakers of America: Their Lives and Works*. Examining cabinetmakers rather than the cabinets they made, Bjerkoe's publication expressed a renewed rigor in the study of American decorative arts following World War II. Bjerkoe operated an antiques shop in Essex, Connecticut, with her husband, and in 1950 published a book on household taste, *Decorating For and With Antiques*. Yet with her second book, she highlighted documentary evidence of American cabinetmaking culled from historical newspaper advertisements, bills of sale, probate records, court records, and surviving furniture.

11 Isabella Ruth Doerfler (1883–1954), *Guilford Blanket Chest*, ca. 1936. Watercolor, colored pencil, gouache, and graphite on paper. H: 11 in. W: 13 13/16 in. Index of American Design, National Gallery of Art, Washington, D.C., 1943.8.4636.

12 Isabella Ruth Doerfler (1883–1954), *Side View of Guilford Blanket Chest*, ca. 1936. Watercolor, colored pencil, graphite, and ink on paper. H: 10 7/8 in. W: 8 7/8 in. Index of American Design, National Gallery of Art, Washington, D.C., 1943.8.4635.

Charles Guillam was a special interest of Bjerkoe's, and she pursued his life story with vigor. Inspired by the then well-known details of his probate inventory, she mined the public records of colonial Saybrook for details of his life, and despite several errors in her research, argued that the painted chests were made entirely in Saybrook rather than Guilford.[13] In 1973, based on the newly uncovered history of a chest in the Tully family of Saybrook who lived adjacent to Guillam, she asserted without qualification that Guillam produced all of the painted chests in his Saybrook shop.[14]

The second important event of 1957 was an exhibition from December 1957–May 1958 staged at the Connecticut Historical Society in Hartford of six painted Saybrook or Guilford chests largely borrowed from private Connecticut collections. William Warren of the Historical Society arranged the exhibit and wrote an accompanying article in the *Connecticut Historical Society Bulletin* titled "Were the Guilford Painted Chests Made in Saybrook?" Through this project Warren attempted to articulate a typology of the chests, grouping together like forms, but he ultimately had difficulty addressing the formal variety seen within the assembled pieces. Although he tempered his language in comparison to hers, he followed Bjerkoe's lead in arguing a Saybrook origin in Guillam's shop for the painted chests on display.[15]

Tellingly, both Bjerkoe and Warren largely ignore the painted decoration on these chests beyond noting that the chests were painted. Bjerkoe described them briefly, while Warren pointedly argued that the, "Tudor rose, Scotch thistle, French fleur-de-lis and the crown" were "obviously derivative from earlier times" and were consequently "of no significance here other than decoration."[16]

Although the painted Saybrook or Guilford chests remained in many prominent collections of American furniture, the next burst of scholarly research into their form and decoration did not appear until the 1990s. In 1994 Martha Willoughby wrote an extensive study of Connecticut chests of the early eighteenth-century while a student in the Winterthur Program in Early American Culture.[17] That same year Robert F. Trent, then curator of furniture at The Henry Francis du Pont Winterthur Museum, published a focused study titled "A Channel Islands Parallel for the Early Eighteenth-Century Connecticut Chests Attributed to Charles Guillam" in *Studies in the Decorative Arts*.[18] Both studies are still important sources for scholars, offering unimpeachably rigorous examinations of the construction of surviving chests, and highlighting important details about the life of Charles Guillam.

Yet both studies also largely neglect questions of style and meaning sitting in plain sight on the surfaces of the painted chests from Guilford and Saybrook. Both Trent and Willoughby mined the Channel Islands heritage of Charles Guillam for European parallels to the Connecticut chests, but such connections are largely superfluous until concrete proof of Guillam's authorship is uncovered. Guillam is linked to these chests largely as a matter of circumstance. Their formal variation in construction and decoration strongly suggests a variety of hands at work, and their histories of ownership place them in different towns. With these facts in mind, it seems more prudent to examine the specific colonial contexts in which they were generated rather than their European phylogenesis.

The present study aims to fill the gaps these prior examinations left in order to present a full picture of the construction, decoration, use, and history of these fascinating chests. The four chapters dedicated to those subjects highlight the complex meanings these chests would have had when they were new, and their modern legacy as icons of American vernacular design. Yet it still remains for future scholars to uncover new aspects of this story and information about the origins of this tradition. Perhaps, as Susan Schoelwer suggests in her introduction, there are undiscovered parallels in the practice of ornamental painting like that seen on Connecticut tavern signs. Perhaps additional sources heretofore unidentified exist in British and Continental painted furniture to explain the distinctive decoration. Perhaps additional historical documents will prove that Charles Guillam or one of his peers constructed these chests. These and other avenues of inquiry may yet yield important new insights.

As new information comes to light, this story will continue to evolve in fascinating ways.

NOTES

1 Henry Whitfield State Museum curatorial files, 59.1919. Guilford, CT.

2 Irving W. Lyon, *The Colonial Furniture of New England* (New York: E.P. Dutton, 1977), 24–25.

3 Briann G. Greenfield, *Out of the Attic: Inventing Antiques in Twentieth-Century New England* (Amherst: University of Massachusetts Press, 2009), 69–70.

4 Henry H. Saylor, "The Best Twelve Country Houses in America IX: Westomere, The Home of George S. Palmer, Esq., at New London, Conn." *Country Life in America* (Jan. 1916), 27.

5 Henry Watson Kent, "The Bolles Collection: The Gift of Mrs. Russell Sage," *Bulletin of The Metropolitan Museum of Art* 5:1 (Jan. 1910), 14–16.

6 Ethel Hall Bjerkoe, "Charles Gillam–Cabinetmaker," *Spinning Wheel* 29:4 (May 1973), 24–25.

7 Malcolm A. Norton, "Chest of Our New England Grandmothers," *The Magazine Antiques* II:2 (Aug. 1922), 76.

8 Norton, "Chest of Our New England Grandmothers," 76–78.

9 Wallace Nutting, *Furniture of the Pilgrim Century* (Framingham, MA, Old American Company, 1924), 45.

10 Gilman C. Gates, *Saybrook at the Mouth of the Connecticut* (Orange, CT: Press of the W.H. Lee Co., 1935), 182.

11 Robert F. Trent, "A Channel Islands Parallel for the Early Eighteenth-Century Connecticut Chests Attributed to Charles Guillam," *Studies in the Decorative Arts* 2:1 (Fall 1994), 77–79.

12 Virginia Tuttle Clayton, "Picturing A Usable Past," in Clayton, Elizabeth Stillinger, et al. *Drawing on America's Past: Folk Art, Modernism, and the Index of American Design* (Chapel Hill: University of North Carolina Press, 2003), 1–7.

13 Ethel Hall Bjerkoe, *The Cabinetmakers of America* (New York: Bonanza Books, 1957), 102–104.

14 Bjerkoe, "Charles Gillam–Cabinetmaker," 24–25.

15 William L. Warren, "Were the Guilford Painted Chests Made in Saybrook?" *Connecticut Historical Society Bulletin* 23:1 (Jan. 1958), 1–10.

16 Warren, 10.

17 Martha Willoughby, "From Carved to Painted: Chests of Central and Coastal Connecticut, c. 1675–1725," 1994. Master's thesis, Winterthur Program in Early American Culture, University of Delaware.

18 Trent, "A Channel Islands Parallel," 75–95.

Martin Partyka (1907–1954), *Guilford Painted Chest* (detail), ca. 1936. Watercolor, colored pencil, gouache, and graphite on paperboard. Index of American Design, National Gallery of Art, Washington, D.C., 1943.8.4677

SELECTED BIBLIOGRAPHY

Arista, Jessica, and Dr. Jennifer Mass, "Technical Study of a Painted High Chest from Saybrook, Connecticut (1710–1727) in the Henry Francis du Pont Winterthur Museum," 2998. Conservation File for High Chest 1957.1110, Winterthur Museum, Garden, and Library.

Belknap, Waldron, Jr. *American Colonial Painting: Materials for a History.* Cambridge, MA: Belknap Press of the Harvard University Press, 1959.

Bjerkoe, Ethel Hall. *The Cabinetmakers of America.* New York: Bonanza Books, 1957.

Bjerkoe, Ethel Hall. "Charles Guillam—Cabinetmaker," *Spinning Wheel* 29:4 (May 1973), 24–25.

Bohan, Peter and Philip Hammerslough, *Early Connecticut Silver, 1700–1840.* Middletown, CT: Wesleyan University Press, 1970.

Buck, Susan L. "Below the Surface: Discovering the Original Paints on a Guilford, Connecticut, Chest," *Historic Deerfield* 11 (Winter 2010), 23–27.

Carter, R.O.M and H.M. Carter, "The Foliate Head in England," *Folklore* 78:4 (Winter 1967), 269–275.

Chesebrough, Harriet Chapman. *Glimpses of Saybrook in Colonial Days.* Old Saybrook: Published by Celebration 3 1/2 , 1985.

Christie's, New York, *Property from the Collection of Mrs. J. Insley Blair* (Sale 1618), Lot 521, Jan. 21, 2006.

Clayton, Virginia Tuttle, Elizabeth Stillinger, et al. *Drawing on America's Past: Folk Art, Modernism, and the Index of American Design.* Chapel Hill: University of North Carolina Press, 2003.

Collier, Christopher. "Saybrook and Lyme: Secular Settlements in a Puritan Commonwealth." *A Lyme Miscellany, 1776–1976.* Ed. George J. Willauer, Jr. Middletown, CT: Wesleyan University Press, 1977.

Cooper, Wendy E. and Lisa Minardi, *Paint, Pattern, and People: Furniture of Southeastern Pennsylvania.* Winterthur, DE: Henry Francis du Pont Winterthur Museum, 2011.

Crawfurd, Raymond. *The King's Evil.* Oxford: The Clarendon Press, 1911.

di Bonaventura, Allegra. *For Adam's Sake: A Family Saga in Colonial New England.* New York: Liveright Publishing Corporation, 2013.

Fairbanks, Jonathan L. and Elizabeth Bidwell Bates. *American Furniture, 1620 to the Present.* New York: Richard Marek Publishers, 1981.

Fairbanks, Jonathan L. and Robert F. Trent. *New England Begins: The Seventeenth Century.* Boston: The Museum of Fine Arts, 1982.

Fales, Dean A., Jr. *The Furniture of Historic Deerfield.* New York: E.P. Dutton & Company, 1976.

Fales, Dean A., Jr. *American Painted Furniture: 1660–1880.* New York: Bonanza Books, 1986.

Gates, Gilman C. *Saybrook at the Mouth of the Connecticut.* Orange, CT: Press of the W.H. Lee Co., 1935.

Greenfield, Briann G. *Out of the Attic: Inventing Antiques in Twentieth-Century New England.* Amherst: University of Massachusetts Press, 2009.

Jobe, Brock, Gary R. Sullivan, and Jack O'Brien, *Harbor & Home: Furniture of Southeastern Massachusetts, 1710–1850.* Lebanon, NH: University Press of New England, 2009.

Kamil, Neil. *Fortress of the Soul: Violence, Metaphysics, and Material Life in the Huguenots' New World, 1517–1751.* Baltimore: Johns Hopkins University Press, 2005.

Kane, Patricia E. *Furniture of the New Haven Colony: The Seventeenth-Century Style.* New Haven: The New Haven Colony Historical Society, 1973.

Kane, Patricia E. "The Seventeenth-Century Furniture of the Conencticut Valley: The Hadley Chest Reappraised." *Art of the Anglo-American Community in the Seventeenth Century.* Ed. Ian M.G. Quimby. Twelfth Annual Winterthur Conference Report. Charlottesville: The University Press of Virginia, 1975.

Kent, Henry Watson. "The Bolles Collection: The Gift of Mrs. Russell Sage," *Bulletin of The Metropolitan Museum of Art* 5:1 (Jan 1910), 14–16.

Kierner, Cynthia. *Traders and Gentlefolk: The Livingstons of New York, 1675–1790.* Ithaca, NY: The Cornell University Press, 1992.

Kirk, John T. *Connecticut Furniture: Seventeenth and Eighteenth Centuries.* Hartford: Wadsworth Atheneum, 1967.

Kirk, John T. *American Furniture ad the British Tradition to 1830.* New York: Alfred A. Knopf, 1982.

Kugelman, Thomas, P., Alice K. Kugelman, et al. *Connecticut Valley Furniture by Eliphalet Chapin and His Contemporaries, 1750–1800.* Hartford: Connecticut Historical Society, 2005.

Lane, Joshua, and Donald P. White III, "Fashioning Furniture and Framing Community: Woodworking and the Rise of a Connecticut River Valley Town," *American Furniture* (2005), 155–166.

Lyon, Irving W. *The Colonial Furniture of New England.* New York: E.P. Dutton, 1977.

Myers, Minor, Jr. and Edgar deN Mayhew. *New London County Furniture, 1640–1840.* New London, CT: The Lyman Allyn Museum, 1974.

Norton, Malcolm O. "Chests of Our New England Grandmothers," *The Magazine ANTIQUES* II:2 (Aug 1922), 76–78.

Nutting, Wallace. *Furniture of the Pilgrim Century.* Framingham, MA: Old American Company, 1924.

Panofsky, Erwin. "What is Baroque?" *Three Essays on Style.* Ed. Irving Lavin. Cambridge, MA: The MIT Press, 1995.

Roberts, William I., III. "Samuel Storke: An Eighteenth Century London Merchant Trading to the American Colonies." *The Business History Review* 39:2 (Summer 1965), 147–170.

Safford, Frances Gruber. "Floral Painting on Early Eighteenth-Century American Furniture at The Metropolitan Museum of Art." *Painted Wood: History and Conservation.* Eds. Valerie Dorge and F. Carey Howlett. Los Angeles: The Getty Conservation Institute, 1998.

Safford, Frances Gruber. *American Furniture In the Metropolitan Museum of Art: 1. Early Colonial Period, The Seventeenth-Century and William and Mary Styles.* New York: The Metropolitan Museum of Art, 2007.

Saybrook's Quadrimillenial. Deep River, CT: Press of Clark & Smith, 1886.

Schoelwer, Susan Predergrast. "Connecticut Sunflower Furniture: A Familiar Form Reconsidered," *Yale University Art Gallery Bulletin* (Spring 1989), 20–37.

Schoelwer, Susan Prendergast. *Lions & Eagles & Bulls: Early American Tavern & Inn Signs.* Hartford: Connecticut Historical Society, 2000.

Smith, Ralph Dunning. *The History of Guilford, Connecticut.* Guilford: J. Munsell, 1877.

Steiner, Bernard Christian, *A History of the Plantation of Nenunkatuck and of the Original Town of Guilford, Connecticut.* Baltimore: Published by the author, 1897.

St. George, Robert Blair. *Conversing by Signs: Poetics of Implication in Colonial New England Culture.* Chapel Hill: The University of North Carolina Press, 1998.

Sweeney, Kevin M. "Mansion People: Kinship, Class, and Architecture in Western Massachusetts in the Mid Eighteenth Century," *Winterthur Portfolio* 19:4 (Winterthur 1984), 231–255.

Trent, Robert F., "A Channel Islands Parallel for the Early Eighteenth-Century Connecticut Chests Attributed to Charles Guillam," *Studies in the Decorative Arts* 2:1 (Fall 1994), 75–91.

Trent, Robert F. *Hearts and Crowns: Folk Chairs of the Connecticut Coast 1720–1840.* New Haven: The New Haven Colony Historical Society, 1977.

Vost, John. "Guernsey Painted Chests." Manuscript provided by the author, 2013.

Vost, John. "Channel Islands or Connecticut?" Manuscript provided by the author, 2013.

Ward, Barbara McLean, Lynn Brocklebank, Catherine Jacobs, et al. *A Place for Everything: Chests and Boxes in Early Colonial America.* Winterthur, DE: Henry Francis du Pont Winterthur Museum, 1986.

Ward, Gerald W.R. *American Case Furniture in the Mabel Brady Garvan and Other Collections at Yale University.* New Haven: Yale University Art Gallery, 1988.

Ward, Gerald W.R. and Willian N. Hosley, Jr., ed. *The Great River: Art and Society of the Connecticut Valley, 1635–1820.* Hartford: Wadsworth Atheneum, 1985.

Warren, William L. "Were the Guilford Painted Chests Made in Saybrook?" *Connecticut Historical Society Bulletin* 23:1 (Jan. 1958), 1–10.

Whittelsey, Charles Barney. *Genealogy of the Whittelsey-Whittlesey Family.* Hartford: Press of the Case, Lockwood, and Brainard, Company, 1898.

Willoughby, Martha. "From Carved to Painted: Chests of Central and Coastal Connecticut, c. 1675–1725," 1994. Master's thesis, Winterthur Program in Early American Culture, University of Delaware.

ACKNOWLEDGMENTS

Thistles and Crowns: The Painted Chests of the Connecticut Shore presents a new perspective on an important vernacular tradition in New England furniture making. Following his extensive study of the iconography and construction of the chests, and a careful review of the existing published record, archival sources, and regional history, Assistant Curator Benjamin Colman argues persuasively that the stories of their creation, decoration, use, and histories are a good deal more complex than previously thought. By doing so, the catalogue functions as an enriching companion to the exhibition, and stands on its own as a significant contribution to the scholarship of American material culture.

Projects of this nature are the work of many hands. The Florence Griswold Museum is grateful to Connecticut Humanities, the state affiliate of the National Endowment for the Humanities, and to The Hartford Steam Boiler Inspection and Insurance Company for their belief in this project and support in its realization. They were joined by a small group of leadership donors, including Thomas and Georgina Russo; David and Mary Dangremond; John and Dyanne Rafal; Charles T. Clark; George and Jane Rapport; Robert and Betsey Webster; and Ted and Pamela Hamilton. Their commitment to American art and culture enables the Florence Griswold Museum to pursue projects like *Thistles and Crowns,* offering new insight into our national and local heritage. In addition, support from the Rudolph and John Dirks Fund of the Community Foundation of Eastern Connecticut, the Arden and Millicent Yinkey Exhibition Fund, and the Nika P. Thayer Exhibition and Publication Fund has been invaluable to the Museum.

The gracious assistance of friends and colleagues at many public institutions was invaluable in studying these painted chests. We owe special thanks to Marie McFarlin of the Old Saybrook Historical Society; Michael McBride of the Henry Whitfield State Museum; Karin Peterson of the Connecticut Historic Preservation Office; Charles T. Lyle of the Webb-Deane-Stevens Museum; Peter M. Kenny of the Metropolitan Museum of Art; Robin Jaffee Frank and Alyce Perry Englund of the Wadsworth Atheneum Museum of Art; and Linda Eaton, Brock Jobe, Rosemary Krill, and Wendy Cooper of the Henry Francis du Pont Winterthur Museum. Thanks are also due to Patricia Kane of the Yale University Art Gallery, and independent scholars Robert F. Trent and John Vost for sharing their wisdom and research.

We are grateful for the contributions of two scholars who have helped give the project its present shape. David W. Dangremond, who has long been associated with the Florence Griswold Museum as a trustee, has written a foreword that gives insight into this subject. Susan P. Schoelwer, the Robert H. Smith Senior Curator at George Washington's Mount Vernon, offers a perspective on the study of Connecticut material culture and suggests some possibilities for further investigation.

At the Florence Griswold Museum, Ben Colman worked closely on this project with Curator Amy Kurtz Lansing, Registrar Nicole Wholean, Director of Education and Outreach David Rau, and Facilities Manager Ted Gaffney to plan the exhibition, catalogue, and associated programs. Jenny Chan and Lisa Yelon of Jack Design provided beautiful graphics for both the catalogue and exhibition. Photographer Paul Mutino successfully captured the details of the pieces illustrated throughout this catalogue.

On behalf of the Board of Trustees and professional staff at the Florence Griswold Museum, I would like to offer heartfelt thanks to each of the individuals, institutions, and organizations that supported the full realization of this project.

Jeffrey W. Andersen
Director